*It will soon be thirteen year~~~~~~~~~~~~~~~~~ the downing of our boat, the Me~~~~~~~~~~~~~~~~~~ be told, but I couldn't do it, and it~~~~~~~~~~~~~~~~~~~ady to entreat my trusted friend wiui un~ ~~~~~~~*

*Everything you will read is true....*

*Throughout the years, filmmakers, journalists, and authors have all approached me with requests to tell my tale. I repeatedly heard the word "inspirational" attached to it and to me, and I hoped someday the telling might even save lives. But I wasn't ready, until now ...*

—Judith Sleavin

# Ten Degrees
# of Reckoning

*The True Story of Survival*

## Hester Rumberg

*Berkley Books*
*New York*

THE BERKLEY PUBLISHING GROUP
Published by the Penguin Group
Penguin Group (USA) Inc.
375 Hudson Street, New York, New York 10014, USA
Penguin Group (Canada), 90 Eglinton Avenue East, Suite 700, Toronto, Ontario M4P 2Y3, Canada
(a division of Pearson Penguin Canada Inc.)
Penguin Books Ltd., 80 Strand, London WC2R 0RL, England
Penguin Group Ireland, 25 St. Stephen's Green, Dublin 2, Ireland (a division of Penguin Books Ltd.)
Penguin Group (Australia), 250 Camberwell Road, Camberwell, Victoria 3124, Australia
(a division of Pearson Australia Group Pty. Ltd.)
Penguin Books India Pvt. Ltd., 11 Community Centre, Panchsheel Park, New Delhi—110 017, India
Penguin Group (NZ), 67 Apollo Drive, Rosedale, North Shore 0632, New Zealand
(a division of Pearson New Zealand Ltd.)
Penguin Books (South Africa) (Pty.) Ltd., 24 Sturdee Avenue, Rosebank, Johannesburg 2196,
South Africa

Penguin Books Ltd., Registered Offices: 80 Strand, London WC2R 0RL, England

The publisher does not have any control over and does not assume any responsibility for author or third-party websites or their content.

PRINTING HISTORY
Amy Einhorn/G. P. Putnam's Sons hardcover edition / February 2009
Berkley trade paperback edition / January 2010

Berkley trade paperback ISBN: 978-0-425-23210-1

The Library of Congress has cataloged the Amy Einhorn/G. P. Putnam's Sons hardcover edition as
follows:

Rumberg, Hester.
Ten degrees of reckoning : the true story of a family's love and the will to survive /
Hester Rumberg.—1st American ed.
p.        cm.
ISBN 978-0-399-15535-2
1. Sleavin, Judith.    2. Sleavin, Judith—Family.    3. *Melinda Lee* (Sailboat).
4. Shipwreck victims—United States—Biography.    5. Shipwreck victims—New Zealand—
Biography.    6. Survival after airplane accidents, shipwrecks, etc.—New Zealand.
7. Shipwrecks—New Zealand.    8. Boating accidents—New Zealand.    9. *Pan Grace*
(Cargo ship).    10. Cargo ships—Korea (South).    I. Sleavin, Judith.    II. Title.
G530.S59R86        2009                    2008033848
910.9164'79—dc22

PRINTED IN THE UNITED STATES OF AMERICA

10   9   8   7   6   5   4   3   2

*Penguin is committed to publishing works of quality and integrity.*
*In that spirit, we are proud to offer this book to our readers;*
*however, the story, the experiences, and the words*
*are the author's alone.*

*For the crew of the* Melinda Lee,

*spirited adventurers all*

*A voice said in my sleep: "Do not delay:*
*Do not delay; the golden moments fly!"*

HENRY WADSWORTH LONGFELLOW
*The Masque of Pandora* (1875)

# Foreword

✻

IT WILL SOON BE THIRTEEN YEARS SINCE MY FAMILY
disappeared with the downing of our boat, the *Melinda Lee*.
I knew the story needed to be told, but I couldn't do it, and it
took me all these years before I was ready to entreat my trusted
friend with the task of writing this book.

In 1993 my husband and I, along with our son and daughter,
set out to live our dream—to sail around the world. For almost
three years we did exactly that. But in 1995 my family and I
were in a devastating collision that took away from me everything in the world I held dear. My back was broken and my
skull was fractured, with some irreversible brain damage—but
none of that compared with the loss of my family.

There were many times when I thought I, too, was going to
die. What kept me alive was the love of my family and the
longing to tell our story.

Everything you will read is true, and while there are terrible portions, as in life, there is also joy and love, adventure and resilience. When tragedy struck, the depth of the despair was almost exactly the inverse of the incredible height of happiness I had always experienced being with Michael, Ben, and Annie.

Throughout the years, filmmakers, journalists, and authors have all approached me with requests to tell my tale. I repeatedly heard the word "inspirational" attached to it and to me, and I hoped someday the telling might even save lives. But I wasn't ready, until now.

I chose Hester Rumberg to tell our story. It was important to me that she had been an experienced oceangoing sailor like me, that she had sailed on our boat, and that she has been a treasured part of our extended family. I respected her professional accomplishments in her field as a radiologist, and then as my spokesperson in the maritime community. But most important, I could express my feelings and thoughts to her when I couldn't tell anyone else, and she always understood. She had the empathy, love, and patience to listen, and the skill, intelligence, and knowledge to tell the story. A talented writer and a cherished friend, Hester has turned untellable circumstances into a powerful and gripping story. She captured my most elusive feelings and put them into words. She pieced together my painful memories and wove them into an accurate picture. She explored the meanings behind the facts without losing the authenticity of the story. She has balanced a story of unfathomable layers with reflective insights, and has given even me a new understanding of some of its features.

Some parts of this story are still too big for me to comprehend, and some of my feelings are still too raw to articulate. When you read the book, you'll know my trust was not misplaced when I chose Dr. Hester Rumberg as the author. If I could have written a book, this would be it, exactly.

—*Judith Sleavin*

*One*

# November 24, 1995

✹

THIS IS NOT MY STORY. IT IS A STORY EMBEDDED IN THE
very fibers of my heart, and it has changed the direction of my
life, but it is not my story. Oh, I've managed to insert myself
into some of its chapters, but I am a long way from being one
of the principal characters. They have been silenced by an enormous tragedy and its aftermath, and have selected me to give
voice to a story that needs telling. I choose to begin the account
on November 24, 1995, but really, that is when the story ends.

On November 23, 1995, all over the United States people were
enjoying Thanksgiving with their families, in their homes. The
Sleavin family celebrated in the cockpit of their sailboat, the
*Melinda Lee,* sailing toward New Zealand. They were about
seventy-five miles from its coast, and they expected to be there
by the next morning. This might not have been a conventional
Thanksgiving celebration, but they were not a conventional
family. The Sleavins had been away from home for almost three

years, and they planned to settle down somewhere in New Zealand for a while. The family, Mike and Judy and their children, Ben and Annie, were in great humor. The weather didn't match the mood of the sailors, though; it was overcast and gloomy, the wind was increasing in strength, the waves were getting larger, and the whitecaps were spraying them with sea foam and salt water. The Sleavins didn't mind. After thirty-three months at sea, they were experienced in the routines, the capriciousness of the weather, and the patience required in ocean passage-making. The Sleavins had crossed thousands of miles of the Pacific Ocean and the Caribbean Sea in a forty-seven-foot sailboat, and after many remarkable adventures, they were approaching their destination.

At 8:45 that morning, they made their usual daily radio contact with other sailboats heading toward New Zealand's North Island. Most voyaging boats worldwide like to make connections on ham and marine single sideband radio frequency networks. Belonging to a network of sailors gives the crew information about other vessels and conditions at sea, and decreases the sense of isolation. These nets also have a safety aspect. Vessels are expected to check in every day at an established time, and if they fail to do so, search-and-rescue efforts may be implemented. The Sleavins were part of a net facilitated by Annique, another sailor circumnavigating the world.

-------------------------------------------------------------------------------

Morning Roll Call

0745 (GMT)

Good morning, Hole in the Net cruisers. It is now 0745 Greenwich Mean Time, and you are listening to your Net Control, Annique, on the sailing vessel RUQUCA. We check in daily at this time. I will call you in turn. If you have any communications for other boats on the net, please make arrangements to move off this frequency when you have connected. First, stand by for any emergency, medical, or priority traffic. Is there any emergency, medical, priority traffic? Come now . . . Nothing heard, so we will begin the roll call.

(Annique)

---

During a roll call, each boat gave its longitude and latitude, course and speed, weather conditions, barometer readings, and estimated distance to the respective harbor. The Sleavins reported they were heading to the Bay of Islands, where they would check in at Opua, the northernmost port of entry into New Zealand. At the end of *Melinda Lee*'s report, Judy alerted Annique that it was unlikely they would check in the next morning; they hoped to be dealing with customs and immigration. Annique wished them well and reported that the sailboat *Aquavit* was already in Opua and eagerly awaiting *Melinda Lee*'s arrival. Judy made arrangements to switch frequencies with *Aquavit*, and signed off the net with "Safe travels to all."

It had been a gray and drizzly day, but nothing could mute the excitement of an imminent landfall. Annie, who had turned seven on October 2, desperately wanted a dog, and since her parents had decided to take a break from cruising, she was really looking forward to the fulfillment of her dream. She wondered if they had the same kind of puppies in New Zealand as they had in California. Her dad told Annie he knew for certain they would come across sheepdogs, trained to guard and herd flocks

*3*

of sheep. Annie's older brother, Ben, piped up, "Hey, let's get some sheep and name one of them Baaahb."

Typically, on an ocean passage the talk was more of which sails needed attention, the country of origin of any sighted vessels, what kind of fish might be caught on the trolling line, and just where they were on their global positioning system (GPS), their charts, and in this infinite maritime world. For the sake of safety, they had strict routines on passages, and everyone obeyed the rules willingly. Ben, at nine years of age, was now experienced enough to help with keeping short watches for ships and weather changes during the day, and he ran a radio net for other oceangoing children. Annie, who had been four when they departed from San Diego, was an old hand at sea, never complaining and quite fearless. She was always amenable to putting on her life jacket and keeping things neat. Her parents were particularly impressed by how she had begun to develop an innate sense of the world without yet understanding an atlas.

As the day ended, the family members began their regular night routines. Annie, with Mike's help, was reading one of her birthday books, and Ben was singing his favorite song, Joni Mitchell's "Big Yellow Taxi." The kids climbed down the stairwell into the cabin below, took off their life jackets and hung them on a hook by the aft berth. Judy followed the children down, and Ben helped her check that all the toys were put away, the dishes cleared up, and the cupboards and lockers closed with bungee cords. The term "shipshape" is bandied about in many homes, where it refers to keeping things orderly and tidy. On a boat or ship it is crucial to have every item stowed and made secure. Even when a boat isn't pitching and rolling, articles can easily become dislodged and turn into flying missiles.

The children stood by Judy as she turned on the single sideband to get a report from New Zealand. Jon and Maureen Cullen operated a professional net from their home in Kerikeri, in the Bay of Islands, offering weather and sea conditions to incoming vessels and monitoring their progress. Judy turned the dial to get Kerikeri Radio.

*"Any boats nearing northern New Zealand wishing to check in, please come in now. Over,"* came a voice from the radio in the dim light of the cabin.

"Melinda Lee, Melinda Lee. *Over,"* Judy responded.

*"Go ahead,* Melinda Lee. *Over."*

*"Our expected time of arrival in Opua is the twenty-fourth at approximately eight A.M. Do you have any information about the worsening conditions we're experiencing? Over."*

*"Thank you,* Melinda Lee. *There are two fronts expected. Winds thirty to thirty-five knots, possibly with gusts up to forty knots from the northeast, seas in the range of four to five meters. Light rain. Any troubles? Over."*

*"Everything fine, Kerikeri Radio. We are sailing comfortably and anticipate no problems over these next twelve hours before we get in. Over."*

*"We will alert the port captain of your impending arrival. Please call him on your VHF radio when you are in range of Opua. Over."*

*"Thank you, Kerikeri Radio.* Melinda Lee *signing off."*

The kids were really excited. Their mommy had been talking to someone in New Zealand! They wanted to be awakened as soon as land was in sight, no matter how early in the morning. Judy promised, and they both scrambled to get ready for bed. Judy went over to Annie's berth in a small stateroom on the starboard side of the boat, just behind the chart table where they did their navigation and radio communication. Annie, in a T-shirt over clean cotton leggings, was ready to snuggle into her bunk.

She told Judy, "I'm so excited about a puppy. You better give me some extra smooches so I can fall asleep!"

After covering her daughter's face with kisses, Judy went forward to help Ben get firmly situated in his berth. His bunk was located forward of the galley and navigation table, in the main salon, the area that was used as a living room when they were at anchor. Just three weeks earlier, while they were in the Kingdom of Tonga, Ben had wanted to celebrate Halloween. Since no costumes were available, he had to be resourceful. He found several rolls of toilet paper and wrapped himself up as the Mummy. He was very successful in the winding, but as soon as he tried to move, it all fell apart. His plan to scare his Tongan buddies fell apart, as well. Now, this last night before reaching New Zealand, he wanted to try again with his cotton blanket, and since they were out of the Tropics, it was finally cold enough. Ben convinced Judy to roll him in the cozy blanket until he got the effect he desired.

"Good night, Mommy, I love you," he said, encased in his tube of blanket.

"Good night, Mummy, I love you, too," Judy replied.

After the good-night kisses, Judy hooked up the lee cloths that were stretched from the berths to the ceiling to keep the children securely in place. They were made of sturdy canvas and ropes that kept the sleepers from falling out of their bunks, no matter what the motion. The canvas portion was open on top and at either end, so that air could circulate easily. Judy leaned over the canvas for one last good-night check, and then went up on deck to join her husband for a bit of quiet time together. Although he didn't quite match her sense of spontaneity, Mike was as loving and playful as she, and he brought her a steadiness by being so even-tempered and calm.

Mike was preparing for the first watch of the night. Judy gave him the weather report from Kerikeri Radio, and they decided to douse the mainsail and raise the staysail. In their experience, in windy conditions, this sail provided plenty of power and kept the *Melinda Lee* balanced and performing well. Mike and Judy walked from bow to stern for the evening's routine inspection of equipment and lights. They completed the checklist and then sat leaning against each other on the cockpit seat cushion. There was an almost effortless affection between them, but even with all the parental responsibilities and small space, they made sure to have time alone. This wasn't an option on a passage, but at anchor families arranged sleepovers for their children. As kids waved goodbye from a neighbor's dinghy for a night away, everyone in the anchorage knew what the parents would be doing. On an ocean passage, they had to manage with some brief caresses while passing each other and a few kisses when they traded night watch duties.

Judy got up reluctantly, knowing she needed rest so she could take over for Mike at one A.M. "I love you, Michael," she said.

"I love you, too, Judith," he replied. They always called each other by their formal names, although almost everyone else called them Mike and Judy.

Judy went below to carry out her own evening routine. She studied the chart and GPS, updated the log, and checked on Ben and Annie. Despite the increasing sea swells, the boat was sailing easily and the children were sleeping comfortably. This was the first passage in three years that Ben had not thrown up, and Judy was looking forward to marking his new equilibrium with a party when they arrived. She liked to mark all of her family's accomplishments with parties. She climbed into the off-watch bunk on the port side, across from Annie's little stateroom, hoping to get three hours of sleep. For Mike, it was down to the serious business of his night watch.

Like the *Melinda Lee,* most offshore cruising boats use a windvane or an autopilot system to steer automatically. Sailors often call them by names such as Helmer or Tillie or Otto because this piece of equipment is better than having another person aboard. The self-steering windvanes are quiet, with no electrical demands. In the most basic system, once the boat is sailing the correct course, the vane is adjusted to keep the sails at a constant angle relative to the wind. If the vane detects a course error or changes in the apparent wind, it transmits these changes to a submerged blade. The blade turns and generates a mechanical force through the lines running from the rudder to the wheel or tiller. The helm responds, and the boat is kept on course.

In most self-steering models, the more the wind blows, except in extreme conditions, the better the vanes respond. They don't have to be fed or cajoled into taking yet another watch; they keep the boats on course day after day, night after night. The crew is freed up to go forward on deck to reduce or change the sails, to scan the horizon for ships, or to monitor overtaking vessels at the stern. In general, windvanes increase the safety factor enormously, not just by doing a better job of staying the course but also by minimizing fatigue so that sailors are alert to any potential dangers.

Mike adjusted the windvane, checked that the staysail was properly trimmed, and confirmed that the navigation lights were on for the night. International regulations required the running lights of sailboats of *Melinda Lee*'s length to be visible from a distance of at least two miles.

Mike scanned the horizon for ships and then tucked himself into the corner of the cockpit. He had written a long letter to his mother from Tonga, telling her his dream had been more than fulfilled; sailing had presented his family with incredible lessons in camaraderie, cooperation, and responsibility. He added that their enjoyment at being together, twenty-four hours a day, had exceeded all his hopes and expectations. He was sure that this experience would bode well for future success as a family wherever they might land.

The Sleavins had left Nuku'alofa in the Kingdom of Tonga seven days earlier to begin this thousand-mile passage. They had waited for a perfect weather window and were rewarded with steady winds and calm seas in the initial stages of the passage. Now, as they were approaching New Zealand, the conditions were definitely deteriorating. On this last night the wind had increased and was gusting up to 35 knots, with seas at least eight feet high. Despite intermittent light rain squalls, the visibility remained reasonable, and Mike felt confident that he would be able to sight any maritime hazards.

Every ten minutes Mike stood up and walked around the cockpit, making a 360-degree scan. From time to time he went forward on the deck, in front of the sail, to make sure nothing was crossing their path. An estimated two thousand containers are lost somewhere at sea every year, and earlier in the day, over the radio, the Sleavins had heard a report that a ship in the vicinity had lost some of its load. Mike and Judy were aware that each container had the dimensions of another sailboat but without the lights and equipment of a vessel or the eyes and ears of a crew. Propelled by the oceans' currents, these containers move about the ocean, independent of their mother ship, difficult to foretell, and dangerous.

Just before one A.M. on November 24, Mike slid open the hatch from the cockpit, leaned over, and told Judy it was time for her watch. She quickly dressed for the cold weather. On top of her underwear and T-shirt she put on a fleece jacket, fleece pants, foul-weather overalls, and a jacket. Over her foul-weather jacket she put on her personal flotation device and safety harness. She also donned a wool hat and gloves, and sea boots. At the navigation station, Judy used the chart and GPS to verify that they were on the correct course, and computed the time when they would turn on the *Melinda Lee*'s radar. Then she went above to the cockpit to exchange information and places with Mike. He reported that he had seen nothing during his entire watch. Judy told Mike that if she didn't sight any ships, and if weather conditions remained the same, she would wake him to begin monitoring the radar around 3:15 A.M., at which time they would be twenty miles from land.

Mike was always concerned about everyone's well-being, and now that they had left the Tropics he was especially pleased when Judy showed off all her layers of clothing. He gave his wife a hug and told her he was ready for some shut-eye. Before

Mike went down the companionway to occupy the berth Judy had just left, he said, as he had done at every watch change for three years, "Anything wrong, call me. If you see anything, call me. If you want to discuss anything, call me."

Alone on deck in the dark, Judy was glad for all the warm clothing. With the steady increase in the wind it was getting colder, and the seas had increased, up to twelve feet high. She was thankful the boat was sailing well and not getting battered by the large swells. Every ten or fifteen minutes Judy stood up and walked around to get an unobstructed view of the horizon and to search for the navigation lights of other vessels.

At two A.M., Judy picked up the binoculars and scanned the horizon deliberately and slowly. She wanted to be the first one to see land, or at least the lighthouse off Cape Brett, the entrance to the Bay of Islands. Also, it was time to go below to verify their position, and she wanted to assure herself that it was safe to leave the cockpit for a few minutes.

Judy stood and moved about the cockpit and completed a 360-degree turn. She carefully looked in all directions, but there was nothing to see. She put the binoculars down and walked around on deck, tethered to the safety lines. It was more difficult to see when there was cloud cover, but it wasn't impossible to distinguish between sky and sea with the varying shades of gray. Much of the time spent on watches was boring, but Mike and Judy agreed early on not to be distracted by reading books. They wanted to be able to respond quickly to any situation, and it helped to have night vision.

They had encountered many vessels over the last three years and knew that a ship's navigation lights could be seen from quite a distance, often as far as ten miles away. As a further precaution, the *Melinda Lee* had a radar detector mounted on the framework of the stern of the boat, with its monitor situated on the chart table inside. The detector would pick up the microwave pulses of a ship's radar within twelve to fifteen miles of them and sound an alarm loud enough to alert everyone on the boat. Tonight they seemed to be alone. There was not a shriek from the alarm or a squawk from either of the two VHF radios. Not a light anywhere in sight. Judy felt confident that, with no apparent danger, it was safe to go below for a few minutes. She went down into the cabin to the navigation area, unhooked her harness and life jacket, and charted their position from the GPS information. She calculated that they had twenty-eight miles to go; in just over an hour she would wake Mike. Within twenty miles of every landfall, one of them would monitor the radar at the navigation table below while the other remained above in the cockpit or on deck.

Judy finished her navigation tasks. She zipped up her jacket, and just as she moved to go up to the cockpit, there was a sound so violent it flung her forward.

BOOM . . . BOOM . . . BOOM.

A fusillade of flying objects. Something struck Judy on the head. Pain. Water everywhere.

## Two

# Ten-Year Plan

✸

MIKE AND JUDY BOTH HAD THE MOST GORGEOUS
smiles. It was something people always noticed later, when they
looked at the photographs of the voyage. Even after twelve
years of marriage, two children, and the challenges encountered during their epic journey, the wattage of those smiles
never diminished. Well, the photographs are a lasting testa-
ment to their bliss.

Judy was born in North Hollywood, where she attended
school. Her father died of leukemia when she was three years
old and her sister, Risa, was five. Her mother, Caryl, worked as
a librarian for Los Angeles County. Caryl later remarried, but
for a large part of Judy's childhood it was the three of them,
and Judy developed a resourceful nature early. She graduated
from Antioch College in Yellow Springs, Ohio, with a bachelor
of arts degree in textile design. She was very artistic, but practical enough to become part-owner of a restaurant right after
college, and she was emotionally well equipped to create a life

of her own. After three years in the restaurant business, Judy decided she was ready for a new experience, and she hitched a ride with a friend to Washington state, where she met Mike.

Mike grew up in Tacoma, the third oldest in a family of six children. His father was an engineer and his mother a successful realtor and a homemaker. In his teen years, Mike loved any job that had to do with children or the outdoors. He and his dog, Flo, were known for their long wilderness hikes. Mike graduated from Western Washington University in Bellingham with a degree in parks management, and moved to Marysville, Washington, to oversee all the activities of a private campground resort.

When Judy arrived in Washington state in 1978, she applied for a job as the recreational director at this campground, and it was Mike who interviewed and hired her. From the job description, Judy expected she would be supervising families and children, and using her artistic skills to entertain them. Instead, she spent her first week doing little besides making stacks of pancakes for the ravenous campers, and she decided to look for other work. As soon as Judy quit the job, her former boss asked her for a date.

Mike invited Judy for dinner and made her a vegetarian meal; he had just completed a vegetarian cooking class. Judy told him that she was impressed, and Mike admitted he had taken the a course to meet women. When Judy asked him if he had in fact met any, Mike grinned and replied, "Now I have!"

Over dinner, Mike revealed his lifetime dream: he planned to sail from Seattle to Hawaii and then cruise through the Hawaiian Islands. On their next date, Mike took Judy out sailing on *Mika*, his Haida 26, the boat he was outfitting for his offshore adventure. He told her he hoped to be able to leave in several years.

The longer Judy knew Mike, the more she wanted to make that trip with him. She was disappointed when Mike told her he needed a crewperson with skills equal to or greater than his own, since he had never sailed offshore. He knew she was funny and adventurous and smart, but he didn't realize just how determined she was.

Judy took a job at a yacht services company, installing marine electronics and varnishing brightwork. Although she became adept enough to earn the title Varnish Queen, she decided she really needed to impress Mike with some blue-water sailing knowledge. It was 1980, still at least a year before he would set sail. Somehow she was going to have to acquire more offshore experience than he had. Judy went around to yacht clubs, marinas, and sailors' hangouts to check out "Skipper Needing Crew" lists. She found just what she needed. The Sloop Tavern in Seattle was initiating the Jack and Jill race from Port Angeles, Washington, to Honolulu, and each team was to comprise one man and one woman. The race organizer's crew member had just quit, and he needed a female to partner with him immediately.

Mike was astounded at Judy's decision to join this race. She had only sixteen days to prepare before departure, never mind the unrelenting, intensive training at sea. But once she convinced Mike that this was what she wanted to do, he helped her prepare. Judy and the captain did not win, but Mike bought a plane ticket, met her at the finish line, and told her that her résumé was perfect. In fact, he told her, he was going to expand his own offshore experience by helping the captain sail the boat home, from Hawaii to Seattle. This would be the tougher trip, against the prevailing winds. When he returned, they signed up for the next Jack and Jill race, to take place in 1982, and in the two-year interlude they outfitted their boat to meet the offshore race requirements and took every course available, from Celestial Navigation to Medicine at Sea.

Mike and Judy completed the Jack and Jill race together in 1982 on *Mika*, their twenty-six-foot sailboat, and then spent three months cruising among the Hawaiian Islands. In an especially romantic anchorage, they discussed a ten-year plan. They would get married, have two children, work hard, save their money, and buy a bigger boat. When the younger of the two children was five, they would sail around the world.

Judy's college degree had prepared her for a career in an art museum restoring old textiles, but with their new plan in mind, she reentered college to study for a degree in civil engineering. Judy received her bachelor of science in civil engineering, and two weeks later, on June 19, 1983, she and Mike were married in Seattle.

Mike was a master of motivation. His modest style and low-key manner belied his tremendous capabilities. He had stayed in park management, but in the private sector. Mike's career in recreational sites sales was rewarding and lucrative, and his boss was already worried that Mike would be leaving in ten years. He had a quiet sense of self-respect, and a respect for others. Mike created a great working environment, and his subordinates held him in the highest regard. He quickly rose to top positions where he managed large teams of salespeople, and his achievements became widely recognized.

Just before Mike and Judy were married, he was transferred

from Washington to California. Several years after that, he was transferred again as a regional manager to Virginia, where Benjamin Timon Sleavin was born on November 3, 1986.

Before Mike and Judy had the opportunity to bring *Mika,* their sailboat, to Virginia and the Chesapeake Bay, a nationwide private campground system offered Mike the position of general manager at its largest facility in California, so they moved again. At six months of age, Ben, strapped and harnessed and tethered in *Mika*'s cockpit, would have his first sailing adventure in the Pacific Ocean off the coast of California.

Now that the Sleavins were settled in southern California with a home and a child, it was time for Judy to find work in civil engineering. She got a job with a firm engaged in the planning, engineering, and surveying of land development. Judy designed the plans for all the sewer and underground water systems, and the grading for the residential and commercial subdivisions for which her firm was responsible in Van Nuys. She became close to her supervisor, Maureen Lull, who was the project manager.

Initially, Maureen didn't realize that Judy was always teasing her. When she asked Judy what she liked best about her new job, Judy replied, "The lunches." It didn't take long for Maureen to realize that she and Judy had the same mischievous sense of humor. The two of them discovered they also shared a love of sailing, and they joined a women's sailing crew to race every Wednesday night in Santa Monica Bay. They signed up for Safety at Sea and Marine Weather classes at Orange Coast College, and on the long drives to class they discussed their other mutual interests in engineering and quilting and children.

Mike and Judy took Ben out sailing as often as possible in

*Mika,* and sometimes after work they took him on their visits to boat brokers. At the Long Beach Boat Show just a week before Ben's first birthday, with yacht brokers all around, Mike whispered to Judy, "Aren't we supposed to have another baby before we buy a bigger boat? Wasn't that part of the original ten-year plan?"

"Oh, yeah," she said, with a sparkle in her eye. "We better go home and do that."

Anna Rose Sleavin was born in Valencia, California, on October 2, 1988, and the Sleavins were thrilled. With two children and two working parents, life became quite hectic. They lived on one salary and saved the other to buy their future boat and to start a cruising fund.

Two years after Annie was born, they spotted an advertisement for a cutter-rigged Compass 47 sailboat that looked perfect. In May 1990, Judy flew to Fort Lauderdale to inspect the boat. She went out into the Atlantic for sea trials, and had a marine survey done. In between, Judy telephoned Mike at least twelve times, to describe the boat's layout, equipment, and performance. Judy thought it was a very functional boat, and well laid out. It had a spacious open interior with three staterooms and two heads, and a very large salon and galley. The deck was nearly flush, with a low trunk cabin and a huge cockpit. It was South African built, and Judy learned that Dr. Christiaan Barnard, the world's first human-heart-transplant surgeon, had bought a similar one. A boat broker in Florida had imported two of these Compass 47 sailboats to the USA. He was so impressed with their design that he named one after his daughter, Melinda Lee, before putting them on the market.

Mike and Judy made the decision to buy the *Melinda Lee* and had it trucked across the country to the Channel Islands Marina in Oxnard, California. Every time they attended a boat show or a cruising seminar, they outfitted the *Melinda Lee* with the recommended and required equipment. They joined the United States Coast Guard Auxiliary and had the *Melinda Lee* inspected by the auxiliary so they could join in any future search-and-rescue undertakings in the Oxnard/Ventura area. They went sailing together and separately to gain enough experience. When there were storm warnings, they notified the Coast Guard that they were going out anyway, to test the storm sails. They took the previous owners, Scott and Kim, out sailing to learn about all the systems. They took Ben and Annie out sailing in order to practice boat handling while keeping an eye on them. The four of them continued to thrive, even with the increased amount of time spent on preparations.

Everything was falling into place as they rang in 1993. They sold *Mika*, their twenty-six-foot boat. They rented out their home for the next five years, boxed and stored their possessions, resigned from their jobs, and organized a homeschooling system for the children with the Calvert School. The Sleavins asked Maureen Lull to be their emergency contact, postmistress, and surrogate banker, and she accepted.

On March 1, 1993, with all the preparation complete and the send-off parties over, Maureen went to the marina for one last goodbye. She slipped the dock lines, and as the *Melinda Lee* moved smoothly away, Maureen waved and waved until she could no longer see her friends' faces or hear their cheering voices.

*Three*

# Beyond Armchair Cruising

✸

I MET MIKE SLEAVIN AND JUDY HERSHMAN IN THE WIN-
ter of 1982, when they were in the midst of preparing for the
Jack and Jill race to Hawaii on their Haida 26 sailboat.

I had never been on a sailboat until I tested the waters with
my boyfriend, John, the year before. We had some spectacular
times on *Shahar*, his sailboat, venturing farther and farther out
in Pacific Northwest waters. I loved the feel of the tiller in my
hand, the solitude of the sea, and the pleasures of exploring islands and coastal areas of Washington and British Columbia.
John began to give me books by authors who had circumnavi-
gated the world in tiny sailboats.

*Shahar* was a Haida 26 sailboat, exactly the same size and
design as Mike and Judy's. Later we learned the two boats had
been built in Sidney, British Columbia, one right after the
other. We made a plan for a double date, to go to a slide show. I
can't remember anything about the topic or the speaker, but
I do remember the feeling of an immediate connection with

both Mike and Judy. The four of us laughed a lot. How could another twosome be so similar in character and sensibilities? I wondered. We would never have met them without our identical sailboats and comparable dreams, but we shared a friendship that did not require the ocean's waves to carry it along.

Judy told me about their plans to participate in the Jack and Jill race to Honolulu. I asked her to tell me all about her previous offshore race. When I found out she had gone with little experience on a three-week voyage with someone she didn't know, on an unfamiliar boat, I was astounded. When I learned the captain had insisted on twelve-hour watches and hand steering all the way, I knew I could learn something about fortitude from this woman.

Mike and John exchanged ideas about structural and safety modifications, and it was easy to see that John was caught up in the idea of getting our own boat ready for an ocean passage someday. When Mike and Judy returned to the Seattle area after the race, they came to my apartment for dinner and to celebrate their engagement. After toasts to their future, we settled down for a slide show of their race in *Mika* to Honolulu. It was a delightful narrative. By the end, it was impossible not to feel that we really knew them thoroughly. After leaving the cold Washington coast and stowing their foul-weather gear, they were naked under their safety harnesses in every picture.

John and I began to prepare our Haida 26 for a trip to Hawaii. We planned to leave in 1984, immediately after our wedding. Judy became my main cheerleader. She gave me explicit instructions on how to provision the small space for the four weeks at sea. She told me canned goods were worth the space and weight, far better than taking a big bag of rice, which would require cooking in precious rationed fresh water. She hid presents on the boat, gave us a pressure cooker, and lent us their life raft. I had never expected to take a life raft on my honeymoon.

So why do ordinary people choose to go to sea—people who are not explorers or part of the merchant marine or Jacques Cousteau associates? Long-distance sailing is popular, and increasingly so with the advent of new technologies. Yet sailboats can be costly to maintain, uncomfortable both at sea and at anchor, and they are certainly the slowest way to get anywhere. So why did the Sleavins hold fast to this idea of adventure for themselves and their children? John and I could appreciate Mike and Judy's lifestyle because of our own experiences; perhaps sharing some of them will help you understand the appeal.

I can honestly say I loved almost every minute of our first long passage. I lost all perspective of time and place. Life at sea was mysterious and exhilarating, or intense and intimidating, or just a lot of hard work when the line squalls came through. On the clear nights, I took pleasure in staring at the stars to get my reference points, and then finding them again on my next watch as they moved through the night sky. When it was wild and squally and moonless, I felt as unsettled as the weather.

John and I were newlyweds who took turns looking after each other's well-being. Trust and confidence in each other flourished. And we were fortunate; we had a lot of fun together. I could completely understand how Mike and Judy had been seduced by the passage-making, and why they were now moving ahead in their ten-year plan.

Certainly, John and I didn't see everything the same way. The first time we had heavy winds and twenty-foot seas, I was quite frightened. I was on watch and the wind was from behind, creating a roller coaster effect. I called John up and we shortened the sails, then put up the storm trysail, and finally took everything down and sailed with bare poles only. John went below to get some rest while I steadied the helm, surfing down a wave into a black trough, and then climbing, climbing, climbing up the crest of the wave. I became exhausted trying to maintain a watch. I couldn't really see, because of the walls of water all around. I found it menacing and interminable. At the end of my three-hour shift I was pulling off my foul-weather gear and John was putting his on. The wind was whipping the sea into a frenzy of mad whitecaps and foam and chaos, and then down, down, down we slid.

John hugged me and said, "Isn't this the most magnificent, awesome sight?"

My log notes for that day read: *"Are we really on the same trip?"*

Rarely are the seas flat on an ocean passage, and despite the comfort it would bring, you wouldn't want it that way. You need the wind; but the wind creates waves. The speed of the wind, the amount of time it's been blowing, and the distance over the water the wind has blown all contribute to the characteristics of the waves. High winds and rough seas, depending upon the direction from which they originate, often impede progress. Even if the winds are steady and moderate and the seas are fairly calm and not knocking you about, you're lucky to cover 150 miles in a twenty-four hour period. And if you sail against the prevailing winds, perhaps fifty of those 150 miles are actually on your course, as you zigzag your way across the ocean.

During our first voyage, at least once each day, at noon, I would unhook the windvane and take the tiller so John could take a sighting with the sextant. To get our latitude, he needed to be able to measure the angle of the sun above the horizon. Both objects could be seen at the same time with the light reflected from the sextant's two mirrors, and then through the eyepiece. But it wasn't an easy task with all the motion. As we reached the crest of a wave, I would attempt to steady the boat for as long as possible. John somehow always managed to hang on to the sextant and the boat to get an accurate sight. Then he would go below to figure out our latitude and longitude and our progress with the nautical almanac, sight-reduction tables, and our reliable clock, while I reengaged the windvane and remained on watch.

We also continuously plotted our position using dead reckoning: estimating where we were by using our course, speed, and the time it was taking to cover a certain distance. There were days of bad weather when it was impossible to use celestial navigation to verify our latitude and we had to rely upon dead reckoning alone.

At two A.M. on July 29, 1984, at the end of our first voyage, I was on watch. I saw the light of Cape Kumukahi on the Big Island of Hawaii—right where it was supposed to be, at the exact time my new husband had promised I would see it based upon the sun and the stars and calculations he had done for more than three weeks at sea. After twenty-three days with not a landmark in sight, or today's technology to confirm our progress, there was Hawaii rising out of the Pacific Ocean. I knew then that my partner had all the navigation skills of Thor Heyerdahl and, I would bet, a much better sense of humor.

Despite some of the challenges we'd faced, we started planning another voyage as soon as we returned. Through their own offshore racing experiences in their Haida sailboat, Mike and Judy knew how seaworthy our twin pocket cruisers were, but they were incredulous that we wanted to take on a two-year New Zealand voyage in a twenty-six-foot sailboat.

We set off again in 1987. My husband wrote to our family: "It's taken us 2½ months to get from Seattle to San Diego: considered excellent progress in the eighteenth century." California was not unfamiliar territory; we had traveled around in more modern modes several times. However ironic it may seem, this drawn-out journey down the West Coast was more akin to the bushwalking that Bruce Chatwin describes in *The Songlines*. We had the opportunity to absorb the distinctive cultural and geographical changes of California as we entered each port. In every area we visited, we hiked or took a bus to find the track of missions that marked the first settlements. And the approach itself, from the sea, inspired us. I cannot describe how thrilling it was running wing-on-wing under the Golden Gate Bridge, knowing what we had accomplished with the wind and our own resources. We often got into the perfect rhythm of the sea on our passages, so perfect that we hesitated to make for land, but, still, every destination was enticing, whether we were tying up in a marina in a city of glittering skyscapes or negotiating the pass of a coral reef.

You can find the perfect dichotomy in cruising: times when you feel total freedom, and times when you feel totally trapped. Once you leave those marinas you have to be entirely self-sufficient. To do that takes considerable preparation. The sailboat must be equipped and organized and deemed seaworthy in any kind of weather. The sailors must be able to handle the boat and sails and equipment. They must be able to maintain that equipment, repair the sails, deal with possible injuries and medical emergencies, and find supplies when there are none at hand. Only a few blue water cruisers (sailors who undertake long ocean passages) would choose extreme sports in their land life, and although they know there will certainly be tests of courage, of stamina, and of patience, few go cruising just to see what a human being can endure.

Although John had made many modifications to the boat, there were things we had to do without, considering its size. One was a diesel engine; we only had room for an eight-horsepower outboard. Mostly we used the wind, because of the very limited amount of fuel we could carry, and indeed both fuel and water were usually inaccessible.

Our water tank had a capacity of a mere fifteen gallons, and this meant using up precious space in the cockpit lockers to carry jugs of fresh water. On larger boats it is fairly easy to rig a rain catchment system, and fortunately for cruisers today, reasonably efficient watermakers are available. We took advantage of the frequent squalls that blew through to have a shower, and when it was balmy, we took the time to wash ourselves, hoping for a bit of lather, with biodegradable dishwashing liquid and a bucket of seawater. Our towels were always damp and crusty with the accumulated salts of the ocean and our bodies. Without the space for an engine or a wind generator or solar panels, we mounted a little generator on the stern of the boat and towed a seventy-five-foot line with an outboard propeller. Our boat speed generated the electricity required to keep our navigation lights on for safety every night, and keep our ham radio operating so we could send our longitude and latitude once a day.

I doubt that there are prenuptial counselors who suggest learning to communicate in Morse code, but we managed to get both marriage and ham radio licenses at the same time. GPS was still not available to civilians, but we did install a satellite navigation system, which we supplemented with the celestial navigation skills gained from our first passage to Hawaii.

It may seem as though we had many restrictions on that little sailboat, but really we felt just the opposite. When we embarked on our second, much longer voyage, we set our pace and destination in line with our interests, bound only by the weather. The large square-rigged ships used in early exploration had great difficulty sailing into the wind. As voyagers observed and increased their knowledge about ocean wind patterns, sea trade routes were established where the winds were most predictable and blowing from a favorable direction. Not all of our own explorations were on these trade wind routes; there were times we didn't mind bashing into seas in anticipation of exotic locales, instead of sailing with the prevailing winds.

We became resourceful and created new ways of doing most things. I learned to fish and to bake a cake in a pressure cooker on top of our two-burner kerosene stove. John learned the name of every fish in fifteen languages and made a mean stir-fry with shark and green papayas. The longest passage we had with no land in sight was thirty-five and a half days. Every three hours of those thirty-five and a half days and nights we switched our situations, one sleeping or reading or repairing an item, the other keeping watch in the cockpit for hazards and ships and weather changes. The confines were small, the lessons and commitment large. Our successes and failures were shared, and our lives inextricably and profoundly connected. We shed our very independent natures for love and friendship and mutual respect.

Every landfall is astonishing, whether the passage has been seven or thirty days. You first get a glimpse of what you think is a low-hanging cloud, but if your chart plotting is correct, that low-hanging cloud becomes the top of a high, lush island rising out of the sea. If your destination is a coral atoll, you have to be particularly aware of your position relevant to your landfall. Most likely you won't see anything but the tops of palm trees, maybe just five miles away, looking like a spiked punk haircut, and only if you time your arrival so the sun is behind you.

We arrived at one such atoll in the South Pacific and carefully made our way through the opening of the reef. We set the anchor and then inflated the dinghy to get ashore. We took our time; we had to row through a coral path. As we neared the shore, we saw a crowd of people on the beach and decided to find a different landing spot, because it seemed to be someone's private property. We rowed toward another spot, only to see another crowd gathered there. I remarked to John that it seemed like a huge population for such a little atoll. We decided we would have to trespass and make our apologies. When we landed, we were greeted by an entire village. The same folks had been following us from one spot to the next, waiting to greet us. They were ecstatic to see us sail in; we were only the second boat in a year to visit. They asked us if we would please come to meet their chief, and even though he spoke only Paumotan, we had a five-hour chat.

In these cruising adventures, you are never a tourist. You are immediately accepted just by showing up. And really, you can't be a tourist, for in many of these places there are no stores, no restaurants, and no generators for an electrical night life. You are the villagers' diversion and they yours. Perhaps you feel so attached to each island because your approach has been from the sea, similar to the first discoverers' approach. You spearfish, you forage for edible fruits, you exchange items, and you provide assistance and supplies. And you are offered the most profound hospitality. In some places, it seems more appropriate to measure the distance between home and destination in centuries rather than miles.

If you picture cruisers as society's dropouts, you might be surprised at how conventional we are, or at least how conventional the lives of most of us have been. John and I met people from all over the world, who had careers as teachers and airline pilots, engineers and homemakers, bankers and mechanics, physicians and boatbuilders. However, these cruisers resist being pigeonholed into or labeled by those conventional categories of economic or professional status, religion, or age. They want to be part of a community, based only upon shared interests and collective skills. They cherish lively discussions and camaraderie rather than debate over national and political divides. Of course there are malcontents, but they are few. Out at sea, even melancholic dropouts have to scramble to keep up with the forces of nature.

The cruising life is typically not a renunciation of lives or issues at home. I would not presume to know or declare all the reasons why people head out to sea, but most of the cruisers we met simply wanted to travel in an independent and self-reliant way. Some sailors recognize that cruising is the only possible way to visit many of the most remote areas in the world. For others it is as much about the journey as the destination, either because of a spiritual connection to the natural world or the love of sailing itself. Some sailors prefer to follow in the wake of the famed French circumnavigator Bernard Moitessier, who spent most of his time on the open ocean in solitude, never caring to sight land.

At sea, you are accountable for every action you take. On land, it is the same. Villagers and cruisers alike subsist on and share whatever is available, and this can present a dilemma. In one atoll, we were asked if we were likely to remain for two months, as they wished. The weather was perfect and the lagoon was absolutely gorgeous, but the weather had been dry for months. If we stayed, we would use up some of the precious rain water stored in the village tank. If we left early to prevent this, we would be ignoring their gift of friendship and an invaluable experience. We stayed for three weeks, until we had not one can of food left in our lockers, not one dusting of flour in our storage bins. We drank the clear juice from the fresh young coconuts to avoid depleting the water supply, and we left behind all our spoons as makeshift musical instruments.

In another instance, in the Marquesas, John and I walked over to visit a family who needed to repair a board. There were children of all ages gathered around, watching John work in the very hot sun, all of them loosely supervised by the oldest sister, Angela. She had three little children of her own, one a baby; there were thirteen family members in all, and I saw nothing, absolutely nothing in their simple abode. No beds, hammocks, cooking supplies, food, utensils, diapers—nothing. But when we got back to our dinghy, someone from that family had left us a giant stalk of bananas.

Every day, in anticipation of seeing Angela, I would stuff my backpack with anything we could spare. She always had something for me, a tapa cloth made from breadfruit bark, the stripped jaw of a feral pig, a bit of shredded coconut. I taught her some English; she taught me some Polynesian words—not too easy for a woman who likes her consonants. Everywhere we went villagers would ask me why I didn't have children. Even with Angela's tutoring, I didn't have the words to explain my own childhood illness and surgeries. Angela was the most curious of all, and I finally showed her my scars to satisfy her probing nature. On the last day, I gave her my backpack, big enough for her to carry the baby, filled with canned milk and powdered eggs, all my soaps and lotions, and soft cloths to use as diapers. She offered me her baby.

Over the years, we rarely felt unwelcome or put upon. Usually the experience was so affirming and the people so warm and generous, it was difficult to leave. Still, there was not one place we visited where I would have wanted to settle forever. Before the sun went down, I was always glad to climb into the dinghy and head back to our boat. Like turtles, we carried our shelter wherever we went, and, like a turtle, I was often ready to tuck my head in for a little privacy.

Mike and Judy had read articles in several magazines about cruising families. The majority of authors wrote that the best time to cruise with children was when they were between the ages of five and thirteen. After that age, no adventures could compete with the company of friends. And while there were some risks, all the information that Mike and Judy gathered revealed it was far more dangerous to take a child in a car on urban roads than out to sea. As we crossed the South Pacific Ocean, we encountered a fair number of families, and most of the children seemed to adjust well to the life. It appeared to be easier for the parents when there was more than one child aboard, and often boats with children would travel in tandem. The children were "boat-schooled" utilizing correspondence courses, with adjunct lessons in navigation and sail trimming for older children. There was always something to learn. Ryan, one of the toddlers we met in Mexico, was carried aboard straight from his birth, and learned to walk on the family's thirty-two-foot boat. With all that motion, he had the calf muscles of Lance Armstrong. And like Mikhail Baryshnikov, whenever he ventured onto land he could walk only on his toes.

*Four*

# Bonjour de Guadeloupe

❀

WHEN THE SLEAVINS STARTED THEIR BIG TRIP IN MARCH
1993, they had detailed charts of the entire west coast of Mexico and decided the number of stops would depend upon how
well the children adapted to overnight sailing. By Judy's birthday on April 7, they had made great progress and were celebrating in Zihuatanejo.

> *Over the last two years we've spent 80 percent of our free
> time preparing for the trip, and it's all been worth it. The
> boat is great, and, more importantly, the kids are doing
> great. They're happy and becoming more self-sufficient
> every day.* —Mike Sleavin, in a letter sent home

A month later, at the beginning of May, John and I flew to
Acapulco, Mexico, for a month of sailing with the Sleavins on
the *Melinda Lee*. We were going to make the passage with

them from Mexico to Costa Rica. We were loaded down with several boxes of equipment and supplies that Mike had ordered, and we took a taxi to the marina where the *Melinda Lee* was berthed. Before we had the chance to ask anyone where to go, Ben and Annie, and then Mike and Judy, came running up the dock to meet us. Everyone looked wonderful and content. They were lean and fit from lugging supplies in backpacks, from walking everywhere, from trimming the sails and pulling up anchor chain. Mike and Annie were a deep brown, Judy a nice tan color, and Ben, who had the fairest complexion, was a rosy pink. Acapulco itself sparkled turquoise, from the water in the harbor to the paint on the hotels surrounding the bay.

It was an easy decision to join the Sleavins: we had kept in close touch ever since returning from our voyage to New Zealand three years earlier, although we lived in Seattle and they lived near Los Angeles, some thousand miles south of us. They had called to tell us when they found the perfect sailboat. In fact, I flew down to visit them and spent several nights on the *Melinda Lee* in Oxnard, California.

When they invited us to join them for a leg of their circumnavigation, we accepted gladly. It was a way to share a small part of their long-planned dream. In the two months since their departure, even Annie, at four and a half years of age, had become an old salt (the term applied to a seasoned sailor). Ben took my hand and my duffel bag and led the way to the dinghy. He was six and a half and ready to sail to Central America.

As we sailed south from Acapulco, we were delighted to see how quickly the family had adapted to their seafaring life, how engaged they were in its activities, and how they stood up to all its challenges. When we reached Puerto Angel, our first stop, we realized a new aspect of cruising: when you are accompanied by children, every door in every village is opened to you immediately. Of course, there were added responsibilities for the parents. Judy and Mike had to provide schooling and guidance and diversions. But even on the Pacific side of Mexico, even so early in the journey, John and I noticed the easy tone of accord and adjustment.

The kids accepted and followed all the rules and regulations. They kept their life vests at the bottom of the aft companionway and put them on before coming up into the cockpit, regardless of how hot and humid the weather. Ben and Annie never went from the cockpit onto the deck without an adult and a safety harness and tether, and never at sea. They always got into their berths willingly when it was announced that night watches were to begin, understanding that the adults needed to pay full attention to the sea.

During the day, each time Ben and Annie came up from below, Judy would smother them with kisses and tell them how much she loved them. Then she would look over at us and say, "Aren't they wonderful? Aren't they gorgeous? Aren't they exceptional?" We would all laugh and nod our appreciation. But there were lessons and responsibilities that went along with all that loving tenderness. Ben, full of goodwill and confidence, would return to the table in the cabin and do his homework. Annie, who wanted to do everything that Ben did, followed him.

"My daddy said your boat is the twin to ours," Ben said one morning.

"The twin to *Mika*, your first boat, not *Melinda Lee*," I replied.

"What is it called?" he asked.

"*Shahar*," I said.

"What does that mean?" Ben asked.

It was a good question. We had done quite a bit of research, and had checked in Grandma Ruth's seven foreign-language dictionaries, but we were stumped. It might mean "moon," we were told, but *Shahar*'s sole previous owner had died overboard in Puget Sound, and his representative was not able to give us any information. We wouldn't have considered another name anyway; sailors are a very superstitious lot, and renaming a boat only brings bad luck. I grew to love the name *Shahar*, with its exotic flavor. I didn't care if we never solved the mystery of its meaning. Even in gale-force winds, I always felt we led a charmed life on *Shahar*.

In essence, out cruising, you become your boat's name, so strongly are you identified with it. Even in a tight-knit sailing community, other cruisers rarely remember your last names, sometimes your first names, but always your boat's name.

"You're lucky your boat was named *Melinda Lee*," I told Ben. "It's easy to pronounce in many languages when you get to all the foreign ports."

"When I talk on the radio, do I have to say, 'This is *Melinda Lee*,' or can I say, 'This is Benjamin Sleavin'?" Ben asked.

"You say, 'This is *Melinda Lee*, this is *Melinda Lee*, do you copy?'" I said. "That means 'Can you hear me, do you understand me?'"

"But we never met the girl Melinda Lee," Annie said, "whose daddy named our boat after her."

"Well, it's a good name, and an old tradition not to change

the name of a boat. When you get back, we'll read *Treasure Island* together. In that book, Robert Louis Stevenson talks about not renaming a boat."

Mike came up with a theory about the name of our boat. "What were the names of the previous owners?" he asked.

"Arne and Diane," John replied.

"Shoot, I thought I had the meaning of *Shahar* figured out," Mike said. "Sharon and Harry."

Ben and Annie both loved watching John expertly gut all the fish we caught. Judy was teaching the children school lessons three hours a day, five days a week, and I asked if there was anything I could do to help. I warned her that I wasn't at all familiar with the Calvert School correspondence course in which Ben was enrolled. Annie tried to keep up with him, although she was too young to participate.

"How about some nautical jargon?" Judy suggested.

"Can't fathom it," I replied.

"You catch my drift," Judy said, grinning.

The next day I explained the names of the ropes on the boats, starting by saying the ropes that went from the *Melinda Lee* to a cleat on the dock were called lines. I told the kids that when they got to the Panama Canal and rafted up to another vessel, a crewmember would ask them to "throw me your lines." Ropes that trimmed the sails were called sheets, and ropes attached to the bow of a dinghy for towing or tying up were called painters.

"Then what are sheets on a bed called?" Annie said.

"And what do you call the guys who paint pictures and walls?" asked Ben.

We discussed fathoms the next day. I told them that the depth of the ocean was measured in fathoms, with each fathom being equal to six feet.

"So if we hang Daddy upside down into the water from a dock, he'll be one fathom deep instead of six feet tall," Annie said.

"Just make sure he knows it's your idea, sweetheart, and not homework," I said.

She looked at me very seriously. She didn't want me to get into trouble. "Okay," she agreed.

"Why can't we stop every night in the ocean?" Ben asked.

John and I explained that the *Melinda Lee* carried only about three hundred feet of anchor chain, and some parts of the ocean were even deeper than Mount Everest was high. Ben was too young at that point to discuss depth sounders and windlasses and scope, but he laughed and clapped when the lesson dissolved into the four adults singing Irving Berlin's "How Deep Is the Ocean? (How High Is the Sky?)." We were definitely in tune with one another.

In the anchorages, other cruisers hailed the Sleavins as we sailed in, and often came by in their dinghies for a visit. There was laughter and gaiety, and many times freshly baked chocolate chip cookies. Mike told us about the birthday celebration for Judy we missed in Zihuatanejo. "There were lots of boats in the anchorage, so we had twenty-one people on *Melinda Lee* for the party. The only problem was the cake I special-ordered. It was supposed to say *Feliz Cumpleaños, Judy*, but instead it said *Feliz Cumpleaños, Lori.* We didn't know who she was, but she was obviously also having a birthday, so we sang to both of them."

One of the visitors told me, "They're so competent. We always want to know where and when they're going next, and then we secretly follow in their wake."

Mike was known for being overprepared. He and Judy had so many spare parts that I overheard a sailor remark, "Going to the *Melinda Lee* is just like going to West Marine." If he had poked his nose into the lockers in the galley, as I did, and seen the year's supply of peanut M&M's and barbecue sauce, he might have thought he had wandered into the storeroom of a 7-Eleven. If he had looked into the galley freezer and seen the hundred yellow, and still feathered, Mexican chicken breasts, as I did, he might have speculated that Judy had a poultry fetish. The cruising community knew that Mike and Judy were always willing to share the fun, the food, their knowledge, and even those spare parts when necessary.

We had chosen to join the Sleavins for this particular passage because they were going to have to cross the legendary and feared gulfs of Tehuantepec and Papagayo. With the children just getting used to the routines and in need of supervision, it would be advantageous to have four adults sharing the watch-keeping responsibilities. These gulfs are associated with low-lying areas of land bordered by high mountains. This topography creates a wind tunnel as the winds are compressed between the mountains from the Bay of Campeche in the Gulf of Mexico into the Gulf of Tehuantepec, which we would cross first. Farther south, there is similar topography, and the wind funnels from the Caribbean Sea across the isthmus into the Gulf of Papagayo. Storm and gale-force winds (we heard anecdotes describing them as high as 70 knots) can accelerate suddenly and unpredictably on the Pacific Ocean side. Sailors wait for days in

Salina Cruz, the southernmost port in Mexico, for a weather window before making this coastal passage.

We, too, wanted to be as prepared as possible. We studied charts of the areas, and the four of us discussed whether to head farther offshore or to hug the coast. We made the unanimous decision to keep two people on watch while crossing these areas, one in the cockpit and the other at the navigation table, studying the radar and GPS. We didn't let the stories told by other cruisers of winds knocking down masts and blowing out sails affect us. We were not casual or arrogant; we had all put in enough passage time to know we could handle what came our way. When the time came, we faced near-gale-force winds, and the boat did remarkably well.

In between those two gulfs, we met fishermen from Guatemala and El Salvador and Nicaragua who came by in their pongas as we sailed along. It was fascinating to see the varied landscape of Central America and to experience the very precise shift in wind direction every evening when the land cooled down to the ocean's temperatures. Whatever the shifts in wind, the sailboat behaved beautifully and I enjoyed learning its systems. It was also luxurious; unlike *Shahar*, the *Melinda Lee* had roller furling sails and self-tailing winches and a cabin I could walk around and stretch out in.

I was simply enchanted with Ben and Annie, and grateful for Mike and Judy's love and friendship. When John and I left the boat in Costa Rica, there were no doubts in our minds that they were all going to flourish. I was already anticipating the marvelous stories that Ben and Annie would tell in five years.

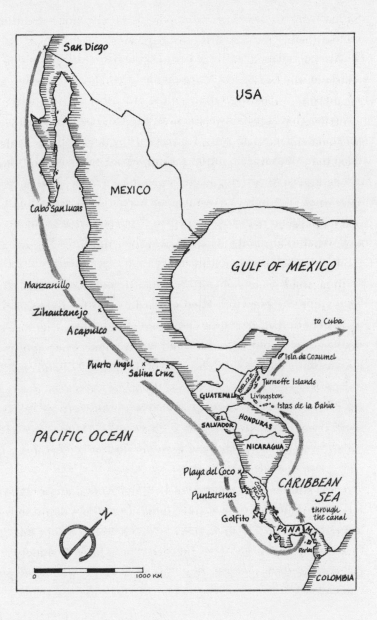

The Sleavins adapted easily to life in Costa Rica. Mike's mother, Catherine, and her friend Marge joined the *Melinda Lee* for a two-week visit, bearing letters, gifts, and more boat supplies. Judy wrote that "the kids were ecstatic to have Grandma twenty-four hours a day, swimming, hiking, sailing, and fishing." She added that "Ben was an emotional wreck for two weeks while his Legos were stowed to make room for boat guests." And Mike described a highlight: "We saw the Arenal Volcano at night with a full moon rising over the top of it. Red lava was streaking down the side, and you could hear the rumblings."

By the end of October, after more than three months of exploring Costa Rica by land and sea, the *Melinda Lee* arrived in Panama. As the Sleavins sailed onward, it wasn't always easy for them to find a port where they could post letters. Whenever possible, they would write to Maureen Lull. She would photocopy the letters and send them to everyone on the group list.

*The southwestern part of Panama has hundreds of islands, each populated with only one or two families. There are protected anchorages and beautiful beaches, and people who love to trade lobsters for T-shirts and toys and powdered milk. We were invited to the birthday party of a five-year-old and had a wonderful time. We arrived at José's grass hut (it was his daughter's birthday) and we were all graciously welcomed. Dirt floors, extremely clean, hand-made furniture, hammocks for beds, lots of smiles and laughter.* —The Sleavins

With all the distractions, getting the kids to focus on school-work was always a challenge. But they were learning to speak Spanish and playing with their new Panamanian friends. Later, the Sleavins sailed to the Balboa Yacht Club, where huge ships making the Panama Canal transit constantly passed within fifty yards of them.

*We just saw the largest ship to ever pass through the Panama Canal, the Royal Princess, a cruise ship that had to pay $141,000 to pass through. We will be transiting in four days, and our tariff is $235.00.* —Mike Sleavin

The Panama Canal traverses the Isthmus of Panama, in Central America, to connect the Atlantic and Pacific oceans. The mean sea level between the two oceans isn't significant, but the locks are needed as the vessels ascend and descend through several artificial lakes and channels from the deep water of one ocean to the deep water of the other. The canal was built mainly for trade, and the first vessel transited in 1914. The Panama Canal has had an enormous impact on shipping; ships no longer have to travel the long and often treacherous route around Cape Horn at the southernmost tip of South America. Nevertheless, the global economy and the subsequent massive ships now being built were never anticipated. The huge ships that Mike mentioned in his letter sent in 1993 are dwarfed by present-day structures, and those that can just squeeze into the canal are referred to as Panamax vessels. On October 22, 2006, Panamanians approved a proposed expansion of the canal in order to accommodate the surge in shipping traffic and the modern ships whose dimensions exceed the Panamax. Tolls are based upon the type, size, and tonnage of the vessels and the kind of cargo they are carrying.

*The transiting of the canal was a wonderful experience. It took two days, and we got to spend the night on Gatun Lake. It is really an amazing engineering feat. We started off crossing through the locks at seven in the morning with an advisor from the canal district aboard. He had a trainee, and it was our responsibility to find the line handlers. Four are needed, so you find two adults from another sailboat at the Balboa Yacht Club, and then you all take the bus back at the end of the transit and help to take theirs through the same procedure. And you bring all the kids with you. We had Dwayne and Debbie from Rubaiyacht and their two kids. Needless to say, it was a full boat.*

*The canal is set up with three locks going up and three coming down. You go up eighty-four feet to Gatun Lake. They have a series of two locks. Then you cross Miraflores Lake, one-quarter mile to the third lock. After coming out, you proceed for eight miles through a narrow channel where only one ship can pass at a time. The cliffs go straight up on each side of you. Ninety million tons of earth was moved from this section. You come out to Gatun Lake, and it is a twenty-three-mile crossing to the down locks. The locks are 1,000 feet long and 106 feet wide. We had to side tie to various ships and boats, although at one point we were squeezed between two large vessels.*

—Mike Sleavin, in a letter sent home

The existence of the waterway had a bearing on the Sleavins' journey. Mike and Judy decided to give their children more time and experience where they were never too far from land, before making a longer passage of a month's duration. By transiting the Panama Canal they could spend more than a year in the Caribbean, with short hops and many ports of call in a variety of countries. They would be able to sail thirty miles between anchorages rather than the three thousand miles required to reach the next landfall in the South Pacific. The family would have a transitional period to adjust to the life, and Ben and Annie's schooling could be expanded with many inland adventures.

Upon exiting the Panama Canal, the *Melinda Lee* headed north. By the end of December, they had spent a month in the Bay Islands, or Islas de la Bahía, of Honduras. Unexpectedly, they had cold front after cold front, with high seas and increasing winds, and they learned to be prepared to leave an anchorage on short notice.

> *Right now we are part of a group of four boats. We arrived in Livingston, Guatemala, after a twenty-four-hour sail from Utila. One by one we were "assisted" over the bar in the Rio Dulce River. All four boats hired a launch to pull down on our spinnaker halyards, from the top of the masts, so that we proceeded into the river at a 20-degree angle of lean. Most interesting way of cruising! Definitely worth it.*
>
> *We're in calm, fresh water full of fish and wildlife. We spent two days slowly traveling up the river, stopping to*

*enjoy a manatee preserve, jungle walk, and incredible scen-*
*ery. Actually that word doesn't do it justice. Pelicans, egrets*
*and ducks flew through the gorge in front of us, 400-foot*
*cliffs on either side, vines hanging down to the water, dug-*
*outs paddling by.* —Judy Sleavin, January 10, 1994

One of the boats in the group was from France, and the
Sleavin family were adding French words to their vocabulary.
Mike was still struggling with Spanish, and Judy wrote about
his favorite joke.

*What do you call a person who speaks three languages?*
*Trilingual. What do you call a person who speaks two lan-*
*guages? Bilingual. What do you call a person who speaks*
*one language? American!*

After two weeks of exploring Honduras and Guatemala by
minivan, Mike and Annie returned to *Melinda Lee*. Judy and
Ben got on a bus headed for the charming little city of Antigua,
the original capital of Guatemala, and also known as La Antigua, for a week of intensive Spanish. By arrangement of one of
the language academies, they lived with a Guatemalan family
and attended classes together. They visited a primary school
and participated in a Mardi Gras celebration with the students.
They visited museums, learned about the colonial buildings and
Spanish-style architecture, and walked among the ruins. They
looked at crafts and watched a renowned and colorful religious
procession. Ben loved all the fun he had with his mom. One
night, after she had answered his usual hundred questions, he
presented her with a ring made of construction paper.

"Someday I'm going to marry you," Ben said.

"Okay," Judy answered, "but it will be our secret. Don't tell Dad."

"I won't if you don't," replied the sleepy seven-year-old.

Every day, Ben bought Annie a present and spent more time shopping than practicing his Spanish. Fortunately, there was a long-winded parrot at the house who liked to yell words at him and Judy, and Ben preferred this style of language acquisition. He was a bit shy about speaking with the Guatemalan family. His grandfather Pops Larry had given him a captain's hat, and Judy suggested that Ben wear it around town to identify himself as a yachtsman. He wore it constantly. He became known by that hat, and was hailed on the cobblestone streets of Antigua as El Capitán Más Pequeño, the Littlest Captain.

In March, the Sleavins sent a letter home with Mike's mother and sister, Sharon, who had come to visit for a week of good fishing and diving. They remarked upon the friendly Belizeans and the gorgeous clean, clear water.

> *Can you believe it? It's already been a year. We've been to seven countries, through the Panama Canal, traveled by boat, bus, bikes, horses, and mostly feet. We've lived twenty-four hours a day together in a small space. We've even had our share of pets: lizards, hermit crabs, lobsters (until the water was boiling). We've come face-to-face with barracudas, dolphins, flying fish, jellyfish, bats, and lots more. It's been a great year.* —The Sleavins

They sailed farther north and met up in Isla Mujeres, Mexico, with Judy's folks and her sister Risa's family, who had come to help her celebrate her fortieth birthday. In addition to the presents, they brought requested equipment and supplies, and the next two weeks were spent on boat maintenance and reprovisioning the galley. The Sleavins' next stop was unusual.

*Greetings from that big island in the Northern Caribbean, the one that starts with the C and is run by the bearded fellow who smokes a cigar. Although officials from five different departments visited the boat to clear us in, there were no difficulties with the authorities. The Cubans have been, by far, the friendliest people we have met. Wherever we walk we carry a large bag of clothes, shampoo and soap, toilet paper, and toys to distribute. We are usually invited in for coffee, and our kids are a big hit, as always. They have been given many gifts, including polished shells, an army beret, a karate manual, thirty pounds of mangoes, and many handmade necklaces made out of plastic, leather, and seeds.*

*We spent three days at Santiago de Cuba, our last Cuban port and the largest city on the southern coast. Entering was incredible. A huge fort/castle from the fifteenth century loomed down on us as our three boats with three American flags sailed into this deepwater bay. Every person we saw— in homes, on boats, on bikes, riding horses, walking—everyone stopped and waved. We look forward to meeting them all, to visiting the museums, and to finding that castle.*

*Annie Rose is now in first grade and Ben has already started second grade. Ben helps Annie with her reading, and today it rained so we made origami frogs and had races. We bought four new Cuban musical instruments, and Ben wants us to have a Family Band and perform in different*

*countries!!! Now there's a child who's watched* The Sound
of Music *too many times.*                    —The Sleavins

When the Sleavins left Cuba to sail to Monte Cristi on the
Atlantic Ocean side of the Dominican Republic, they had an
exciting adventure, at least for Ben. Haiti and the Dominican
Republic share the island of Hispaniola. The Sleavins' route to
pick up their next visitors, Maureen and Richard Lull, in the
Dominican Republic, would take them close to the United
States' naval blockade of Haiti. The embargo made for a diffi
cult passage. They maintained a course outside the blockade,
but they were frequently summoned on their VHF radio, with
stern warnings from the navy to head even farther offshore.

Sailboats made of wood or fiberglass require more than the
mast and rigging to give a good signal on a ship's radar. Adding
a radar reflector, or even several, high up on the mast can sig-
nificantly increase the visibility. That night was a good test; it
was obvious that the radar reflector on the *Melinda Lee* was effective and their radar signal was significant, because each time
they were warned about entering the blockade space, the naval
operator was surprised to be communicating with someone on
such a small craft.

At some point, Mike disengaged the windvane and steered
the boat, while Judy sat in the cockpit with one of their hand-
held VHF radios. Repeatedly, they had to identify themselves
and give thorough details of the crew, vessel, and route. Soon
after one such call, although they were more than twelve miles
off the coast, they saw a huge naval warship steaming toward
the *Melinda Lee.* Judy tried to keep the anxiety out of her voice
over the VHF radio.

"We have two small children who are not able to sleep because of the many disturbances. Is it possible to ask you not to board us? Over."

"Ma'am, we are heading toward your position, and we will deploy one of our inflatables and come alongside. Over."

"Sir, we really are not carrying contraband of any kind. Over."

"Ma'am, we do not plan to interrupt your voyage for any length of time. Do not reduce speed. Stand by on radio. Over."

Ben was ecstatic; the warship was immense, and the inflatable it sent over was almost as big as the *Melinda Lee*. The navy crew on the inflatable pulled up beside them, saluted, and told them to remain calm.

"Sir, ma'am, youngsters. Our admiral asked us to come by to give his regards. He has the utmost respect for a family on a sailing vessel out to see the world. We will not be boarding, but we would like to ask your permission to leave behind some presents from the admiral and his staff."

The crew handed over a bag filled with a month's worth of candy bars, more than five hundred pieces of Legos, comic books, and a signed nine-by-twelve glossy color photograph of the naval ship that read, "Proud to share the seas with the *Melinda Lee*, enjoy your Haitian vacation."

After two weeks in the Dominican Republic, the Sleavins headed toward the island groups in the Caribbean that reflected the historical colonial dependencies and their cultural diversity. Judy and the children were ready to slow the pace a bit, although Mike viewed the upcoming myriad anchorages as ideal pit stops on a race course.

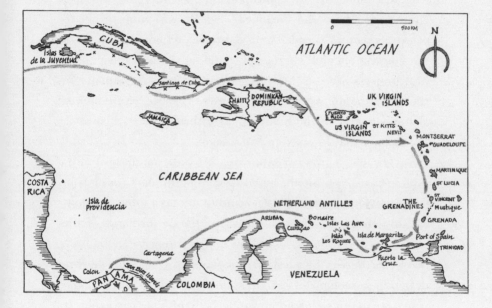

*Bonjour de Guadeloupe! Comment ça va? I'm writing this letter from Les Saintes, a small group of islands just south of Guadeloupe. We're flying our French courtesy flag after muddling through Spanish for the last eighteen months.* —The Sleavins

The Sleavins sailed on to other French islands, as well British and Dutch territories, and had almost completed their circumnavigation of the Caribbean Sea. It was time to get to countries such as Trinidad and Venezuela, where supplies were more accessible and where they could do the necessary major boat projects prior to their long passage across the equator to the Southern Hemisphere. And there were basic requirements, as Judy noted, "We did finally make it through the 186 rolls of toilet paper that I stowed in San Diego."

In Trinidad a group of sailors made a bulk purchase of antifouling paint, commonly called bottom paint. Any boat left in the water for an extended period accumulates a growth of marine organisms. This has an impact on the performance of the propellers and rudders, as well as on the integrity of the hull. Soon, too, there is the question of safety, as the boat slows down, dragging the colony on its underside. One powerboating magazine describes it as having an underbelly of shag carpeting. If standard antifouling paint isn't available, resourceful fishermen find substitutes. For example, in May 2006, while marine scientists were puzzling over the deaths of hundreds of bottlenose dolphins that had washed up on the beaches of Zanzibar, the fishermen there were cutting out the dolphins' livers to use as antifouling paint. Usually their bottom paint came from the livers of sharks, not so easily attainable.

Mike and Judy hauled *Melinda Lee* out of the water in Puerto La Cruz, Venezuela, for all the necessary boat maintenance projects. They also decided to buy a new inflatable dinghy. The dealer would accept only cash. Judy went to the bank. She needed $1,100 for the purchase, and the largest Venezuelan denomination was a four-dollar bill. Perhaps it was because of the recent devaluation, but crime was rampant, and Venezuela seemed lawless to the Sleavins. All their shoes were stolen the first night. They knew a cruiser who had a necklace pulled from her neck, and they saw a robber take a leather jacket off someone's back on the street at gunpoint. Guns seemed to be a common part of life there; they were visible everywhere, sticking out of pockets, dangling from the handlebars of bicycles. In fact, the Sleavins were the only family in McDonald's who didn't lay their guns down on the table before picking up their *hamburguesas.*

Although the dinghy dealership was in line of sight of the bank, it seemed a long way to go carrying hundreds of bills. The man behind her in the teller line asked if she was from *Melinda Lee*, and told her that he was also a cruiser. Did she need an escort? he wondered. They stuffed all the bills down their shirts and pants and in their underwear, and made it safely back to the shop to complete the transaction.

Mike's mother, Catherine, and brother, John, came to visit in Venezuela. They all visited the world's highest waterfall, Angel Falls, hiked through the area, and then drove to the Andes.

When they returned to the *Melinda Lee*, it was particularly difficult for Judy to say goodbye to one couple who were heading back to the United States, Peter and Glenda Couch, on the sailboat *Lamorna.* They had shared adventures for eight months and become like family. As sad as it was to bid farewell, it was also one of the great things about the cruising community: the closeness and the willingness to fill a surrogate role. Glenda ran the radio net and cut everyone's hair, but she and Peter had a more important role in the Sleavins' lives: they were Ben and Annie's offshore grandparents. Glenda was impressed by the determination with which Mike and Judy were raising the children. They wanted their children to have social interactions and adventure, but school always came first, the Couches observed. In the environment of anchorages, where everything was fascinating and spontaneous, the Sleavins insisted that the children understand their responsibility to schoolwork before play and gratification.

The Sleavins sailed west, reaching Colombia in time for Christmas. From Colombia they sailed to the San Blas archipelago, and then to Panama. They sailed over to the yacht club in Cristóbal, where they planned to do all the paperwork required to transit the canal. Also, Mike had made arrangements to have an updated version of the emergency position-indicating radio beacon (EPIRB) shipped to the yacht club. He wanted to replace their 121.5 MHz model, whose range and accuracy were limited, with a 406 MHz EPIRB, which provided global coverage for search-and-rescue purposes.

COSPAS-SARSAT is an international organization, sponsored by Russia, the United States, Canada, and France, that oversees a system that detects and locates transmissions from emergency beacons carried by aviators and mariners, and recently climbers and other individuals, anywhere in the world. From its inception in 1982, it is credited with providing assistance that has saved more than twenty thousand lives. When an EPIRB (an ELT—emergency locator transmitter on aircraft) is activated in a distress situation, its signal is received by one of a network of low-earth-orbiting satellites and high-altitude geostationary weather satellites. The satellite downlink signal is then relayed to the nearest available ground receiving station, where it is processed to find the location from which the signal originated. The Mission Control Center organizes the remaining data. All EPIRBs must be registered, and once the unique identification code of the beacon's owner and relevant information is known, the location is verified. The center notifies all the appropriate rescue centers based in the geographic location. Mike hoped they would never have to activate their new 406 EPIRB, but it gave him peace of mind for the upcoming month-long passage. Even in the middle of the ocean, with its worldwide coverage, the COSPAS-SARSAT system would be able to determine the signal's position within three miles. With the new EPIRB onboard the *Melinda Lee,* the Sleavins were ready to re-transit the Panama Canal and cross the Pacific Ocean to the legendary South Seas.

They found line handlers at the yacht club in Cristóbal and paid their toll, which included the service of a professional pilot. At Limón Bay, the start of the transit on the Atlantic side, the *Melinda Lee* was directed alongside a large ship, and when everyone's lines were secured the massive lock gates swung shut. Millions of gallons of water filled the lock, allowing all the vessels to float upward. They were in and out of three locks that lifted *Melinda Lee* eighty-five feet before they motored over to Gatun Lake. They had an easy sail across the twenty-three miles of the lake, but Ben and Annie were surprised to see alligators lounging in the water. On their first transit, going the other way, they had gone swimming in the same lake, unaware that the tropical jungle held creatures who might be interested in them. They anchored for the night and in the morning continued on, through the Galliard Cut and over to the Pedro Miguel Locks. They were lowered to Miraflores Lake and the Miraflores Locks, where they went down farther to sea level. The lock gates were opened and whoosh, they were in the Pacific Ocean.

*We hit the two-year mark. Can't believe it's been that long and this much fun. So now the real excitement begins; the biggest and longest passage of our trip is about to happen, 3,800 miles to the Marquesas. A boat our size should average 100 miles a day, taking into account the lighter winds near the equator. The doldrums. Thirty-eight days and nights is a looooong time with two kids in 47 feet. I've had the kids memorize parts of "The Rime of the Ancient Mariner," a ritual for the equator crossing.*
—The Sleavins, March 1995

The average person who previously took no notice of longitude and latitude is now familiar with expressing locality in degrees and minutes and seconds because of the popularity of the global positioning satellite system for the car and even personal wristbands. When you reach your destination with the aid of your GPS, you don't really care how far you are from the equator or Greenwich, England, but in fact, that is just what those numbers denote. The latitude is the angular distance of a point north or south of the equator (zero degrees latitude), and the longitude is the angular distance of a point east or west of Greenwich, which is referred to as the Prime Meridian (zero degrees longitude). All the lines of latitude running from the equator to the North and South poles are parallel to one another and equal in distance. One degree of latitude is equal to sixty nautical miles. The lines of longitude run perpendicular to the lines of latitude and are referred to as meridians. They are not equal in distance, but get closer together toward the poles, where they converge.

At sea, the accuracy of those coordinates can mean survival or not, especially in the South Pacific Ocean, with hundreds and even thousands of square miles of water between landmasses. The early sailors developed navigation skills by observing the patterns of the waves and the blueprints of the skies during their voyaging adventures. Later came the active use of celestial navigation in exploration; ships could determine their latitude by tracking the sun's position throughout the day, and the North Star or the Southern Cross by night.

With instruments that were the precursors to the sextant, the sailors' knowledge of their location in a north or south direction became even more accurate. Nevertheless, until well into the eighteenth century there were shipwrecks and lost crews by the multitude, because there was no reliable way to determine longitude. After John Harrison, an English watchmaker, solved the problem with his marine chronometer, Britannia ruled the waves, and the rest, as they say, is history. With the current satellite-dependent technology, such as GPS, it is almost impossible to miss an island completely or, conversely, to run smack onto a coral reef or into a rocky coastline.

Notwithstanding the ease of knowing just where you are in a vast ocean these days, reaching the latitude of 00 degrees, 00 minutes, 00 seconds is still as celebrated as it was in the old seafaring tradition.

Those who have never crossed the equator at sea are termed "pollywogs," and must undergo initiation rituals in order to enter the domain of Neptunus Rex. Any crew members who have made the transition are termed trusty "shellbacks," and can ask the 'wogs to perform whatever elaborate ceremonial rites suit them. Judy was the only shellback as the *Melinda Lee* crossed the equator; years before, when she had completed high school, she spent a Semester at Sea set up by the Institute for Shipboard Education.

Judy insisted that her three pollywogs dye their hair red, paste on temporary tattoos, make brownies for her, and perform several sea chanteys. They belted out parts of "Popeye the Sailor Man" and "Jamaica Farewell," and Mike even managed to sing "The Wreck of the *Edmund Fitzgerald.*" Then one last thing, the recitation of a small portion of Samuel Taylor Coleridge's *The Rime of the Ancient Mariner*:

*Down dropt the breeze, the sails dropt down,*
*'Twas sad as sad could be;*
*And we did speak only to break*
*The silence of the sea!*

*All in a hot and copper sky,*
*The bloody Sun, at noon,*
*Right up above the mast did stand,*
*No bigger than the Moon.*

*Day after day, day after day,*
*We stuck, nor breath, nor motion;*
*As idle as a painted ship*
*Upon a painted ocean.*

*Water, water, everywhere,*
*And all the boards did shrink;*
*Water, water, everywhere,*
*Nor any drop to drink.*

Ah, the doldrums. Many folks think of it as a state of mind rather than an actual area. If you're at home and you're in the doldrums, you might be down in low spirits or listless. However, if you're at sea, near the equator, you might be trapped in the doldrums, where the prevailing northeasterly trade winds of the Northern Hemisphere meet the southeasterly trade winds of the Southern Hemisphere and they neutralize each other. Most cruising sailors try to prepare for these windless days by storing additional provisions and water, bringing interesting books to distract them from the anxiety of the lack of any progress, and attempting to sail a course close to a longitude where the band of the doldrums is somewhat narrower.

If you ever want to feel entirely alone, sitting on a boat in the midst of a becalmed sea is the way to do it. As the narrator in *Moby-Dick* remarked, "The horizon floats," and it is an apt description. You feel as though you can see to the ends of the world, and you're the only ones in it. Everything shimmers in the heat and stillness. The days can multiply without a breath of wind.

In 1988, when John and I were becalmed for some days near the equator, I was absolutely mesmerized by the silence, enthralled by the beauty, and peaceful—not anxious—in the tranquillity of it all. At my suggestion, to abate his restlessness, John was wrapped up in one of the only mystery novels he ever read, one in which, unfortunately, the detective passionately describes another cold beer or ale every few pages.

I was making lunch and threw the onion waste overboard. In less than a minute a shark, with two remoras attached, shot up from the deep. The shark got bored with us fairly quickly, but not before quelling our desire to cool down with a swim. We hung a line over the side to measure the depth of its reflection in the water as it appeared smaller and smaller, and we were sure we could still see its diminished form at seventy-five feet.

Several hours later, John threw our dinner overboard, for simple entertainment value, and the same shark torpedoed back up, the remoras still attached. At the time I didn't realize I would soon become accustomed to swimming among sharks in the many anchorages we visited. They would hang around, uninterested, until they smelled the blood of a fish on the end of our speargun.

The doldrums are more properly called the Inter-Tropical Convergence Zone. The convergence of the prevailing winds of the Northern and Southern Hemispheres, as well as the intense heat in this area, can result in totally unpredictable weather, from the calms to confused seas and countercurrents. On that crossing in 1988, John and I, both pollywogs, dressed up in our two lightweight, colorful spinnakers and beseeched King Neptune to let us enter his domain. We were swept into a wind tunnel before we could properly stow our initiation garb. On a second crossing in 2001, we encountered only thunderstorms and lightning, with skies black day and night, and no chance to celebrate the equator's charisma.

Fortunately for Mike and Judy and the children, their crossing was uneventful, with light winds throughout the equatorial belt. Ben and Annie, hair dyed red, tattooed, and tethered, went forward on deck with Mike to make sure there really was no line in the ocean.

The Sleavins had a great passage to French Polynesia. It took a total of thirty days of sailing, and Ben and Annie became completely accustomed to the routines. They visited the Marquesas for one month, and then went on to the Tuamotu Archipelago.

*When we left the Marquesas we started getting into very squally weather with high winds of about 40 knots and 8-foot seas. We had to slow the boat down so that we would arrive at the coral pass of Manihi in the Tuamotus in daylight. To do this we had to deploy a Galerider, a huge net type drogue that slowed us down by 3 knots. The Galerider made it more comfortable, but that's our version of comfortable.*
—Judy Sleavin

Most of the islands and atolls they visited were much more isolated than their Caribbean stops, and they had exceptional experiences.

*Hello from Tonga. Today I realized how different it is cruising in the South Pacific compared to the Caribbean. I was watching my beautiful little girl have a long discussion with an older Tongan man. In the Caribbean there were more distractions. It was easier to mail Ben's schoolwork for evaluations. There were airports to bring in and take out visiting friends and relatives. There were many more boats and anchorages and tourist activities. In the South Pacific, we have interacted as a family even more, if that's possible, and we have definitely had more association with the people who live in the various places we have visited.*

*That is apparent by Annie Rose's easy familiarity with this man. He paddled by in a canoe, and he had just the shell that Annie wanted to get for Ben's birthday coming up in November. Can you believe it? Annie just turned seven and Ben will be nine in a few weeks. So, back to the shell. The Tongan man was warmly welcomed aboard the Me-linda Lee and offered juice by Annie. She began the negotiations by asking all about his family, and then produced gifts for him that were just right: shoes and clothing for his family, proper fish hooks for him, a board that might be a hindrance to the pigs that routed out his small dirt garden, and some cans of food with an opener. He produced the most gorgeous horned shell, and she had the most incredible smile on her face. She has carefully wrapped it in several*

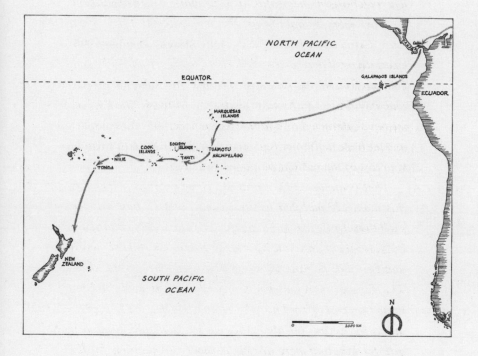

*towels to disguise the shape and has hidden it away for the big day.*

*Also, Mike has gotten much more involved in teaching the kids. He is painstaking in his reading and writing with Annie. I love to watch Mike and the kids when he takes them out in the little sailing dinghy in a protected anchorage. I can hear them laughing as he teaches them the intricacies of tacking and jibing.*

—Judy Sleavin, October 1995

Two weeks after Ben's ninth birthday the Sleavins prepared to leave. They had to wait several more days for favorable weather conditions, and on November 16, 1995, they departed from Nuku'alofa. They expected that the thousand-mile passage to New Zealand would take about a week.

*Five*

# The Littlest Captain

❀

JUDY OPENED HER EYES. PAIN. WATER EVERYWHERE. IT could only have been a few seconds since she'd been hit by some flying object, so why was there so much water in the watertight cabin? She saw floating debris, diesel fuel, a large piece of teak. It took several minutes before she understood that something must have collided with them, tearing a gaping hole in the hull and letting all this seawater in.

She was completely alert now, capable of quickly assessing the damage. The sailboat was equipped with starboard and port diesel tanks located under the settees. It was getting murkier and more difficult to see, but as diesel fuel continued to spill into the cabin, it appeared to come from the tanks on the port side. Her stomach churned. They had taken this massive hit forward. Below the settees was where Ben slept. She fought to keep her panic down, but she knew, she *knew*, that it would have been impossible for him to survive.

Judy screamed, "Michael!" There was no reply.

"Michael!" she screamed again. Nothing. Her head was still slightly above water, but she was aware that she had little time before she would be entirely submerged.

The deck hatch, which had been closed and latched, was missing, and she managed to swim up through the opening to the deck, looking for her family. When she got topside, she found Mike and Annie, completely dazed and holding hands, shivering. The deck was awash, already up to Annie's knees and rising fast. Wreckage was everywhere; Ben was nowhere.

Mike and Judy looked at each other, terror in their eyes. Annie was frantic with worry over her brother. Mike decided to get her safely into the life raft and then attempt to find Ben. He went forward to the mast, where he expected to find the life raft. He was stunned; there was nothing to deploy. There was little left on the deck. The mast was sheared off to a jagged six inches; the rigging, the stanchions, the shrouds, the navigation antennae, the solar panels, all were gone. The life raft had been securely installed in a custom-made teak base bolted through into the cabin top with stainless steel backing plates, and somehow it, too, was gone.

Forward on the deck, a partially deflated dinghy was the only thing remaining, its fifty-foot painter clipped to a U-bolt. Under normal conditions, the dinghy was used to transport the family a short distance from an anchorage to land. Fully inflated, it measured eleven feet by five feet, and it was comfortable and sturdy. However, whenever Mike secured it on deck for a passage, he took some of the air out of the tubes in order to fold it. It was made of a very durable rubber, and he hoped, even partly deflated, it would be buoyant enough to help them until they were rescued. At least it would provide some fortification against the icy waters. As Mike pushed the dinghy over the damaged rail, Judy thought she saw a large dark hull turning away from them, but she couldn't be sure. Ships were always brightly lit with their multiple navigation lights, but she didn't see any evidence of even reflected light on the seas near this hull, if that's what it was.

"Michael, look. Is that a ship?" she asked.

Mike replied that he couldn't see any lights, and he instructed Annie and Judy to get in the dinghy.

Annie was screaming, "Don't leave him. We can't leave without Ben."

Mike told Judy to get in the dinghy; he intended to swim below and get Ben.

Judy became hysterical. She begged, "Please, Michael, please. Don't. You'll never be able to find him. I can't bear to lose both of you. There is no cabin. There's nothing but seawater and diesel and rubbish below. Please! We're sinking fast!"

Most of the hull of their sailboat was now submerged, and the deck was level with the seas, which made it easy for the three of them to scramble into the dinghy. The painter was still attached to the yacht. Almost immediately the *Melinda Lee* sank, pulling them underwater as well. They were screaming for Ben and for themselves, and then the painter broke free, and Mike, Judy, and Annie surfaced in the dinghy.

They could not believe how quickly the seaworthy *Melinda Lee* disappeared. But their own survival was far from triumphant with the horrible, incomprehensible, sickening awareness that the Littlest Captain had gone down with his ship.

*Six*

# Abandoned by Grace

✦

FOR A FEW MINUTES THE THREE WERE UTTERLY SILENT, in a state of shock. They sat in the bottom of the dinghy, completely still, and the dinghy, too, was almost motionless, silently bobbing in a pool of diesel fuel.

Judy completely understood Mike's desire to make every desperate effort to search for Ben, but she had been the last to swim up from what was left of the cabin. It had been so full of water; she had to follow some tiny air bubbles to find her way up to the deck. Mike had been awakened abruptly and hadn't yet fully absorbed the extent of the damage. She knew he would have ended up trapped. And she simply couldn't bear to lose her husband as well.

The dinghy flipped and tossed them out. Mike and Judy righted it, and Mike helped everyone get back in. They were all thoroughly soaked. In spite of the wild seas beyond them, the dinghy was still in a zone of calm water, surrounded by diesel fuel, so it didn't make sense when they flipped again, and then again. Each time it was more difficult to climb into the dinghy, with their bodies heavy with salt and diesel, and limbs less agile from the cold.

Judy became aware of an excruciating pain in her back and needed Mike's assistance. She knew something had hit her on the side of her head when she was still down in the cabin, but she couldn't understand what had happened to her back.

She was glad they were close to land; she was less worried about her injuries than about Mike and Annie's well-being. They had no physical injuries, but their scant nightclothes were already sodden with salty seawater and they were soaked to the skin.

Mike put his arms around Judy and Annie, although he was really the one most in need of tenderness right then. Judy's mind raced back to all the teasing she had taken from Mike's siblings at their wedding, about making babies immediately. They had told her that as soon as he was old enough, Mike became a camp counselor, that he had always loved children. He had babysat willingly; he had helped teach Little League Baseball; he simply loved being involved with children. When Ben and Annie were born, he was overjoyed, and he never felt beset by the responsibility. Leaving a child behind was against his very nature.

Mike and Judy had established special bedtime rituals for the kids whenever they were at anchor. They would each spend time with one child and then switch after lengthy discussions or prolonged reading sessions. Judy once asked Annie what were the happiest and saddest times she could remember.

Annie had answered, "I don't know, Mommy, because I always feel so happy."

Ben had more complicated things on his mind. "I really want to know why songs get stuck in my head," he said once, and another time, "Where does God come from?"

Thinking of this now, Judy gasped in anguish. Who would ask her all those questions now? She wondered, too, in the face of Ben's death, if Annie's once indestructible spirit would be muted. She wondered if any of them could ever return to their normal selves, their normal lives, their normal routines. Mike had always liked to be the first one awake when the family was in a pleasant anchorage with settled weather. He would stealthily get up from the forward berth, pull on his shorts, and make coffee. Then with his cup and a book, he would head out to the cockpit and sit under the awning. Even though he tried to get up without waking any of the others, Annie would always hear Mike and join him. Each morning they sat in the cockpit and watched the sun come up together.

On those same mornings, in the sheltered anchorages, Judy and Ben both loved sleeping late. When they awakened, they would make pancakes together, singing and planning the new day ahead. Ben was Judy's "little man," always wishing to emulate her. It was excruciating to be without him. And thoughts of Ben trapped in his cozy blanket, as the Mummy, unable to free himself, kept intruding and tormenting Judy. All Judy wanted at that moment was to wallow in her grief. But it was up to her to move on to the next step and make sure that the remaining family survived. She had to figure out why the dinghy kept flipping, so she could warm up Mike and Annie, and pass on some of her clothing to them.

It was a pitch-black night, but Judy's eyes began to adjust to the darkness all around. She took a good look at the state of the dinghy. There was very little air in it, and Judy wondered if it could actually carry them toward land. She took off her sea boots and began bailing out the water in the dinghy when Mike turned his head, exclaiming, "Look! Judith, you were right. It was a hull you saw, and the ship is returning! It must be the bow wake that keeps flipping us."

"Are you sure, Michael? How can you tell? I don't see any lights," Judy replied.

The ship's silhouette could barely be seen, it was so dark. Then suddenly they saw faint lights and the shadowy side of a large ship, perhaps only seventy-five feet away. The lights were not the bright navigation ones they were used to observing on big ships, but three rows of dim lights like the accommodation lights of a passageway and crews' quarters. On two of the upper decks they could see faces, perhaps nine or twelve of them, pressed against a large window. The faces appeared to be peering out and looking straight at them, but no one moved. There was no one on the bridge or at the bow of the ship using searchlights.

Mike, Judy, and Annie got on their knees in the shaky dinghy, waving madly and shouting, "Help us, help us, please help us!"

To their horror, the ship continued on. There was blackness again, the dark hull disappearing, no lights at the stern at all.

*Seven*

# Rules of the Road

✴

WHAT KIND OF SHIP WOULD LEAVE TWO ADULTS AND one tiny girl frantically waving and shouting for help? What kind of crew would fail to use the required navigation lights to be seen, then fail to use searchlights to discover what destruction they had wreaked? What kind of a captain would ignore the responsibility to assist by every possible means? What kind of shipping company might give instructions to continue on their way?

We presume a certain order in our lives, whether instituted by the rules and regulations of our respective governments or guided by human decency. We wouldn't want to leave our homes for work or school if we didn't think it possible to arrive safely and make it through the day alive. But if just one person in our path drives on the wrong side of the road or brings a weapon to school, then our chance of survival diminishes.

In the open ocean there is an established body of laws,

the International Regulations for Preventing Collisions at Sea (known as COLREGS). These regulations and agreements have evolved over centuries. As early as 1836, there were parliamentary committees appointed in England to inquire after the causes of shipwrecks, and the first international conference of maritime nations was held in Washington, D.C., in 1889. In 1914, two years after the loss of the *Titanic,* the first International Conference for Safety of Life at Sea convened.

It may seem in the vastness of the seas that there is unlimited visibility, but often ships just over the horizon cannot be seen because of the earth's curvature. While there are no shipping lanes out at sea, there are advantageous navigation routes where it is likely that vessels will, and do, encounter one another. Consider that the oceans cover three-quarters of the globe, and it makes sense that shipping is the most practical way to transport most of our goods in this global economy, with an estimated fifty thousand ships out at any one time. In addition to the professional mariners and those sailors who choose to see life from a small yacht, there are approximately nine million cruise ship passengers a year who choose to take their vacations and explorations on the water.

The International Regulations, known informally as the Rules of the Road, apply to all types of watercraft and take into account every measure to avoid the chance of collision.

It is required that every vessel have a proper lookout at all times, by sight and by sound, as well as any other available means, so that early and substantial actions can be taken well ahead of time to avoid collisions.

Every vessel must proceed at a safe speed in order to be

able to slow down or stop within a distance that will prevent a collision.

Every vessel must exhibit lights from sunset to sunrise, and in conditions of poor visibility. There are specific requirements for the location of lights, depending upon the type of vessel, and the distance and direction of visibility, depending upon the length of the vessel. To be seen calls attention not only to the vessel's position but also to its direction of travel and whether it is under sail or power.

Every vessel must understand its obligations when one vessel is overtaking another, or when two vessels are meeting head-on, or when two vessels are in a crossing situation. At sea, where there is vast turning space, the responsibilities are determined by one vessel's position relative to the other. For instance, in a crossing situation, the vessel that has the other on its starboard (right) side is obliged to keep out of the way, and is called the give-way, or burdened, vessel. The other vessel is obliged to hold course and speed, and is called the stand-on, or privileged, vessel. There are situations where it might be easier for the stand-on vessel to alter course, but only after a discussion on the radio between the two vessels, in order to understand the intention and thus avoid chaos and collision. In narrow channels or confined areas such as harbors where large ships have little maneuvering capability, recreational sailboats and powerboats must not impede their progress.

There are additional rules, including those applying to communication and sound signals, especially when there is danger of a close encounter.

If everything should fail, and two vessels are involved in a collision, there are separate regulations. Under international maritime law, vessel masters have an obligation to render assistance to those in peril at sea.

Without Ben, there is no argument: life could never be the same for the Sleavin family. But if the captain of the ship had provided assistance to two adults and one tiny girl in distress, the story would have ended here.

# Eight

# Grave Impact

THIS WAS NOT POSSIBLE. THE SHIP HAD DESTROYED their son and their home, and now it was continuing on without them. Mike started yelling as loudly as he could, "Damn you, you bastards, come back and get us!"

With no lights at the stern of the ship, it was difficult to see its course, but Judy knew it was moving farther away from them.

Mike waved his fist in the air and screamed more loudly, "Damn you to hell, you uncaring bastards! Come back and see what you've done!"

Judy said quietly, "Please don't swear in front of Annie." As she spoke, she was thinking about how irrational she sounded, how ridiculous to pretend that this was a casual remark in a regular everyday conversation. Here they were, without Ben, abandoned in a dinghy, and she was trying to protect her daughter's ears from a slight profanity because she couldn't protect her from this hideous, staggering ordeal.

Annie wasn't paying attention to either of them.

"Where's Ben? Where's Ben?" she kept screaming.

Judy wrapped her arms around Annie, all of them sobbing now, and told her as soon as they were rescued they would talk about Ben always and forever.

Annie was cold. Judy took off her foul-weather jacket and put it on Annie. It was large, but she pulled the hood firmly around Annie's head, and the Velcro cuffs around her small wrists. There was an elastic belt built into the jacket, and Judy cinched it tightly. She told Annie to keep her legs crossed like a pretzel.

Mike was shivering in his underwear and a sweatshirt. Judy wanted to give him her foul-weather pants. She thought she would be warm enough in her polar fleece layer, and she was worried about him. She tried to get her pants off, but her legs were numb and there was little room to maneuver in the dinghy.

"Give a tug, Michael. I can't get these overalls off without your help. And you need them," Judy insisted.

He refused. "I need the two of you to stay warm. Don't even think of getting out of those pants," Mike replied.

Judy had cause for concern. It was the end of November, the beginning of the summer months in New Zealand, and fortunately the water was warming up. Still, the temperature was probably about 14 degrees Celsius (57 degrees Fahrenheit) with stormy seas ahead. Given Mike's state of undress, and the fact that he had been tossed into the ocean three times already, any prolonged exposure in these conditions could cause hypothermia.

The wake of the ship must have pushed the dinghy from the pool of diesel into the nearby waves, and they were moving with the seas. This was the inflatable dinghy that Mike and

Judy had purchased in Venezuela just before they made their return Panama Canal transit. It had a hard fiberglass bottom in anticipation of all the coral reefs in the South Pacific. But it was woefully inadequate compared to the life raft that had been swept away. The life raft was well built, with a protective canopy and an effective ballast system. The life raft was stocked with food, a medical kit, fishing and safety equipment, paddles, flashlights, signaling mirrors and recently purchased flares, even a hand-operated watermaker. The inflatable dinghy they were left with was like a little rubber raft, meant for scooting around a harbor.

One side of the dinghy, the most deflated side, was almost flush with the surface of the waves and didn't provide any barrier at all. Seawater poured in. Mike and Judy used her boots to bail vigorously, but they couldn't keep up with the deluge. Rocked by the last of the ship's wake and swamped with water, the dinghy flipped yet again, and tossed them into the freezing ocean. Instead of trying to get back in, they decided to leave the dinghy overturned. They would have a better chance of sitting or lying on top of the fiberglass bottom. Mike and Judy got on either side of Annie, and clinging to the upside-down pontoon area, they made their way around the perimeter. The painter, a long rope used for towing or securing a dinghy to a dock, was purposefully strong, and Mike pulled it across the bottom to the stainless steel eyebolt on the other side. Judy tied it securely and used it to pull herself up onto the hard bottom. With Mike pushing Annie from behind and Judy pulling under her arms, they got her out of the water. Judy made sure Annie was grasping the painter tightly, and then she helped Mike pull himself up. They had to sit low on the hard bottom in order not to slide off, but even with the pitch, it was preferable to the constant swamping. They had a tight grip on the painter, huddled together with their hands over each other's for a bit of warmth and comfort. It was far from perfect, but it was their only means of reaching land—that is, if the current cooperated. The seat, the oars, and the outboard motor had all been stowed for the passage, so they had no means of propelling themselves in the right direction.

The dinghy was carrying them along despite the high seas, but Mike was shaking uncontrollably, and Judy was enormously concerned. It was a sign of his body's futile attempt to produce heat, but it also foretold of worse signs of hypothermia: confusion, delusions, and mental impairment as the temperature in his brain cooled, and even heart failure if his deep-body temperature cooled down enough. He was such a responsible and protective husband and father; he couldn't bear to take any of Judy's clothes, whatever the consequences to him.

Mike was consumed with guilt about not grabbing the EPIRB. It was mounted in the aft cabin, easily reachable from the off-watch bunk. During their preparations, they had had so many discussions about where to place it, and had decided the children might accidentally activate it if it was mounted in the cockpit. Now the EPIRB was trapped in the submerged boat instead of broadcasting its distress signal.

In November 1995, there were three low-orbiting satellites in the COSPAS-SARSAT system. Had the *Melinda Lee*'s 406 EPIRB been activated, most likely within two hours the Local User Terminal near Wellington, New Zealand, would have received and processed the satellite downlink signal to generate distress alerts. This information would have been forwarded to the Australian Mission Control Center to organize the data about the registered owner and the vessel. New Zealand maritime authorities would have then been alerted to mobilize search-and-rescue efforts.

Over and over Mike kept muttering that he should have grabbed it.

Judy said, "You know what? We're not going to talk about what we don't have. It's way more important that you grabbed Annie."

"Don't worry, Daddy," Judy remembers Annie saying. "Annique will talk to everyone on the Hole in the Net and start a rescue for us. Don't worry, Daddy, Annique is going to save us."

The three locked themselves together, their bodies entangled, sitting low. They would crawl, as one, back up to the high side of the dinghy if the waves caused them to slip downward. Mike and Judy kept their hands over Annie's little ones, as they grasped the painter. They passed Annie back and forth between them, cradling her in their arms. Judy marveled at her little daughter's strength and spirit. In spite of being cold and frightened, Annie didn't complain. For a long time, she kept chattering. She tried to help Judy cheer Mike up by telling stories, but he remained unresponsive and indifferent. He wasn't even mentioning the cold any longer. They named all the cousins, all thirteen of them. Annie told Mike she had thought of a name for her puppy. It would be called Sparkie. They sang a Hebrew prayer, the Shema, and prayed. Mike had never been a remote father, and Annie began to huddle closer to Judy, perhaps sensing that she had a better chance for survival with her mother.

After a while, Annie became quiet. Judy started reconstructing all the events in her head. She knew their position minutes before the ship rammed them, and she made herself remember everything that had happened since the collision. Mike shifted a little, and Judy thought he was trying to make himself more comfortable. He took each of their hands, raised his head, and seemed to see them clearly for the first time in hours.

"I think we should join Ben as quickly as possible," Mike said, in his most rational voice. Still holding their hands, he slipped into the water, deliberately pulling them with him.

Judy and Annie were shocked that they were back in the water, but before they could even speak or cry out, Mike continued, "We'll dive down as far as we can, still holding hands. Open your mouths, let out your breath, and take in as much water as possible. Keep doing it so your lungs can fill. You'll panic at first, but just for a minute, and then you'll feel good. We'll open our eyes and look at each other. We'll be holding hands and we'll go to heaven together and join Ben."

Annie was terrified. She could barely keep her head up. "Daddy, why won't we stay on top of the dinghy and try to go to New Zealand? Daddy, please, I don't want to die."

Annie was wailing, Judy was weeping, and yet Mike seemed calm, almost bewildered by their reluctance to participate in his plan.

Somehow Judy and Annie managed to get back on the dinghy and pull Mike up as well. Judy knew he was weakening rapidly; this behavior was in complete opposition to his normal self, especially as a protective father. He wasn't clearheaded, and as he was only in underwear and sweatshirt, his physical and mental impairment could only worsen. Mike began to mumble, and to ask Judy to repeat things over and over. He seemed so unsettled. Judy started singing softly, and Annie joined in. Judy knew Annie was equally devastated, but they discussed poodles and Bernina sewing machines, hoping to encourage Mike to hang on.

Later, the New Zealand National Meteorological Service (MetService) would reconstruct the weather data in the area. They would estimate winds at 40 knots and seas up to 7 meters (21 feet). The dinghy was not built for these conditions. On top of their little rubber boat, the wind seemed to come from everywhere, as the Sleavins were tossed across the enormous swells. Water rushed over them, walls of water. They were terrified and mute; in the shrieking winds, it was useless to try to holler at one another. They huddled close.

Darkness gradually turned into a gray dawn. They had survived the night. For six hours Judy and Annie had each kept a tight grip on Mike's hand to keep him attached to the painter and to them. It was Annie who saw the sailboats heading toward shore.

"Look, Mommy, there are our friends!"

Judy was battling exhaustion and frustration. They had been so well prepared. They had kept an abandon-ship bag and a waterproof VHF radio in a watertight bag, handy at the bottom of the aft companionway stairs. Seawater had filled the boat in seconds, and everything had gone down with *Melinda Lee*. Now Judy had no means to hail these sailboats or call attention to their presence. She didn't want to frighten Annie.

"I see, Annie, and you know what? We're heading to land, too."

It was true; normally the prevailing winds were westerly, but with these northeasterly winds, they were being carried toward their destination. It was still very overcast, and the wind had not abated at all, but at least it was light out. Annie's excitement raised Judy's spirits, and the two of them made a game of counting and naming the sailboats. Mike was reluctant to even raise his head, but at least he wasn't unconscious.

"Look, Michael, look up! That must be Cape Brett and the entrance to the Bay of Islands, with boats heading in to Opua."

It was fortunate they were this close to land, because Mike seemed completely disoriented, and Judy feared he would lose consciousness.

Just as Judy was beginning to feel encouraged about their progress, the wind shifted and propelled them backward, forcing them away from land. This was disastrous. Mike needed immediate medical attention. And they all needed to be retrieved from the dinghy as soon as possible. She wanted to be heading the same way as the incoming sailboats. She wanted to be in their paths. How else would they be rescued?

Judy checked her watch: nine A.M. She had another disheartening thought. Annique would have hailed them on the Hole in the Net by now, but Judy had told Annique not to expect a response on the morning roll call. She had said they would be busy with customs and immigration. No one would be alarmed yet. On the positive side, Annique had hooked Judy up on the radio with Erica Crenshaw on *Aquavit*, already in Opua and waiting for them. She also remembered she had told Kerikeri Radio they would check in with the port captain at approximately eight A.M. Judy knew that the cruisers always expected the *Melinda Lee* to arrive early.

She estimated their distance at about ten miles from Cape Brett, but whenever they got closer to land, the current and seas would sweep them back out. She forced herself to remain calm. Of course they would be rescued. They wouldn't have to spend another night on the dinghy. She was certain Annique would be on the radio in a few hours in order to establish their safe arrival. *Aquavit* would inform the net of their absence and alert everyone else in Opua, by that afternoon at the latest. Judy felt somewhat relieved; they could hang on until then.

The wind continued to propel them away from land. An hour went by. Another front developed and the winds increased to gale-force strength. The waves were huge and confused, lumping up every which way and making it difficult to hang on, but they all managed, clutching the painter as the dinghy climbed the vertical walls of water. With each wave Judy thought, *This is the end.* But the dinghy went over the top every time, and she thought, *Wow, some kind of miracle.* But then she saw it: the huge curling wave coming toward them, foaming white at its crest before it broke, crashing into them. It hurled Mike, Annie, and Judy off the dinghy in opposite directions.

They had always had a safety routine, in their snorkeling adventures. If the wind picked up or the sharks got too close, Judy would pull up the little anchor and ready the dinghy, and Mike would gather the children. Now, whether he was, in his mind, back in an anchorage on a family outing or was truly aware of the peril in the present circumstances, Mike responded as he always had to any risks.

"Quick, Judith," he yelled, "swim to the dinghy and grab it. I'll go get Annie."

Judy used her upper body to dog-paddle madly over to the

dinghy. Fortunately it wasn't too far away, because she noticed her legs wouldn't function at all, even with the buoyancy of the water. She snatched the dinghy as it rode down a wave and held fast to it, trying to keep her eyes on Mike and on Annie. Mike was definitely the family's best swimmer, but her strong, athletic husband looked like he was swimming through quicksand, sluggish and completely uncoordinated.

Annie was crying out, "Mommy, Mommy, come and save me. Mommy, save me!"

"Hold on, Annie. Hold on. Daddy's coming," Judy shouted back.

Judy was out of her mind with fear. Mike was making progress, but it seemed so slow. Judy was too far away to rescue Annie, and her legs felt useless now. She would have to leave the dinghy behind to get to Annie, and Annie would need the dinghy to survive. With the seas getting larger, Judy was losing sight of Annie, but only intermittently, and only for a few seconds. Then the bright red foul-weather jacket would come back into view and Judy would unclamp her jaw. Please, God, she was praying, we need help.

Another huge wave humped up and rushed toward them. Judy saw Annie rise high up. She thought there was a chance Annie might be thrown toward Mike, but instead she heard Annie choking on all the seawater. Could she actually hear Annie choking, she wondered, or was this her imagination? Choking at least meant Annie was still breathing. Annie's arms began flailing, and Judy watched as the arms of the red jacket thrashed about, then slowed, and then stopped moving altogether.

Judy began screaming. It was not a human sound.

Mike heard those screams and looked over at Judy, just as he was approaching Annie. Then he turned to see Annie, floating facedown and limp. He gathered her in his arms, and even from afar Judy knew by his manner that Annie was no longer alive. She could only guess what entered Mike's distraught and delirious mind, but she knew that Mike was too broken up, physically and emotionally, to cope with the idea of another dead child.

Mike was still holding on to Annie's lifeless body, and they were being carried by the waves in one direction while Judy and the dinghy were being carried in the other. Judy could still see them. It looked as if Mike was kissing Annie's face. And then he let her go. Mike turned back to look at Judy. It seemed to Judy that they stared into each other's eyes for the longest time, and then Mike threw her a kiss. He waved goodbye, and disappeared underwater.

## Nine

## Obligations and Procedures

✸

FOR CENTURIES, SEAFARERS HAVE CONSIDERED IT AN obligation to assist fellow mariners in danger. There have been many remarkable and sometimes heroic efforts made to save lives, regardless of nationality and status.

In 1956, the Italian luxury liner the *Andrea Doria* and the Swedish American Line's passenger ship the *Stockholm* collided. Radio communications had improved by then, and they were able to put out a distress call. Another passenger liner, the *Île de France*, turned back from its own crossing to Europe to provide assistance. Because of this response, and that of several other smaller ships, only five crew members from the *Stockholm* died, and only forty-six of the 1,706 passengers and crew from the *Andrea Doria* perished, despite calamitous damage.

Tradition has evolved into, and is protected by, international law. The International Maritime Organization (IMO), which met for the first time in 1959, is a specialized agency of the United Nations devoted to maritime affairs. Over the years the IMO has developed protocols and recommendations dealing with maritime safety. The details of search-and-rescue obligations are found in various IMO Conventions.

The United Nations Convention on the Law of the Sea, or UNCLOS, says, in part, that every country must require the master of a ship flying its flag to render assistance to any person found in danger of being lost at sea and to proceed to the rescue of persons in distress.

The Search and Rescue (SAR) Convention of 1979 recognizes wider involvement. There is an obligation not only to "retrieve persons in distress and provide for their initial medical or other needs" but also to "deliver them to a place of safety."

The Safety of Life at Sea (SOLAS) Convention says: "The master of a ship at sea which is in a position to be able to provide assistance, on receiving a signal from any source that persons are in distress at sea, is bound to proceed with all speed to their assistance."

In November 2002 there was another nautical hit-and-run in the same area as the *Melinda Lee* collision. The abandoned Swedish yachtsman was fortunate. The collision did not damage his life raft and he had time to send out a distress signal before his sailboat sank. Six vessels, including other sailboats and commercial ships, answered the call for help. Three hours later a Russian ship made it to the scene, and the captain managed to maneuver his 21,000-ton ship around to protect the life raft so that his crew could rescue the freezing, shaking man.

In June 2003, when a dangerously ill crew member had to be evacuated from a sailboat in the North Atlantic, a Greek tanker, a U.S. Navy supply ship, and a helicopter all came to his aid. The rescue was coordinated by the Automated Mutual-assistance Vessel Rescue system (AMVER), which is sponsored by the U.S. Coast Guard. It is a voluntary ship-reporting system used worldwide by search-and-rescue authorities. The Greek tanker was contacted from the center in Norfolk, Virginia, and asked to divert course. Had a vessel been in distress in the eastern part of the North Atlantic, the center in Falmouth, England, would have coordinated all efforts to rescue the crew.

The AMVER system was also used to coordinate search efforts in May 2002, when two Belgian sailors activated their EPIRB from a sinking sailboat. Their mast had broken, puncturing their hull and partially submerging their boat. The crew members of an Indian bulk carrier steamed to the scene and rescued the sailors 470 miles southeast of Halifax, Nova Scotia.

On July 20, 2002, a Japanese fishing vessel grounded on an atoll 330 miles southwest of Wake Island in the Pacific Ocean and was taking on water. The U.S. Coast Guard station in Honolulu requested aid from vessels in the area. An American ship 220 miles and ten hours away diverted course and headed south to rescue the stricken fishermen on the life raft.

The motivation for these rescue efforts, and for the many more not cited, often comes from the long-standing ethical and traditional culture of seafarers rather than from international law. In the open ocean, everyone is a citizen of the same community.

At this point, in the absence of details about the cause of the collision, Ben's death might be attributed to an accident, negligence at worst. But Mike's and Annie's deaths could only be called negligent homicides. A man with no protective clothing and a fifty-pound, seven-year-old girl survived almost nine hours in frigid waters in a deflated dinghy on high seas, abandoned by the very ship involved.

And so I repeat over and over the question that haunts me: What kind of ship's crew would ignore its responsibility to use searchlights or deploy a small launch if they had any inkling that the ship had struck something? Even if the ship's officers chose to ignore the Laws of the Sea that obligated them to render assistance, why could they not at least have contacted New Zealand authorities by radio to report whatever they thought might have happened, and given the authorities the position of the "incident," before continuing on their course? They were only twenty-eight miles from shore. Mike, Annie, and Judy could have been rescued in a timely manner.

"May I forgive myself," said the mythical Captain Ahab on his ship the *Pequod*, just after he had refused to assist in the search for the missing twelve-year-old son of the captain of another ship.

"Do to me as you would have me do to you in the like case. For you too have a boy, Captain Ahab," beseeched the distraught father.

As those many readers familiar with Herman Melville's novel know, Captain Ahab's obsessive pursuit of Moby-Dick precluded any ethical behavior on his part. In his efforts to hunt down the whale and avenge himself, it is a wonder he was even aware that he might have to forgive himself for his repellent act.

Was the captain of the ship that rammed the *Melinda Lee* on his own quest? Not the irrational hunt for a whale, surely, but perhaps a bonus if he brought his cargo to his home port in time? Or did the economic standards of the shipping company itself preclude any delays? Did pride, denial, or inexperience come into his decision? Did he ask himself for forgiveness as Captain Ahab did? Or even feel the need to ask for forgiveness?

*Ten*

# Oceans of Sorrow

❋

JUDY CLUNG TO THE OVERTURNED DINGHY, IN A STATE far beyond shock. Ben's death, the inhumanity of the ship's crew, the relentless attack of wind and waves—nothing prepared her mind and body for this next onslaught. She was in a state of suspension, unaware of where she was, unaware she was even alive. It was the red jacket rising on the seas that brought her back. Judy was drifting even farther away from Annie, but she could still see the red jacket. She ached to go to her, to kiss her goodbye, to do anything to make her trip to heaven easier. She might have a chance, dog-paddling her way to the body, if she didn't drag the dinghy along. But she needed the dinghy to get to shore, to tell someone what had happened, so that she could die in peace and join her family.

She could hear herself screaming still, although the sounds seemed to come not from her lungs, but from a place so deep inside her soul and her guts and her heart that she couldn't make herself stop. When she thought she might be able to get

to Annie to embrace her one last time, she slipped off the dinghy into the water, clutching the painter, riding the waves. It
took her two hours to get back on the inverted dinghy. Two
hours of screaming and wailing and struggling. Two hours of
bile rising in her throat. And because of the red jacket, Annie's
body was distantly visible for those two hours.

Finally, she managed to position herself on top of the dinghy's hard bottom. She could see land in the opposite direction
of the red jacket, so now it really was time to say goodbye. Her
cheeks were soaked with tears, and the wind and the rain lashed
at her face. She noticed vaguely that she was bleeding from the
wound on the side of her head. There was pain, too, but it was
impossible to distinguish the pain of the injury from the pain
in her heart. Funny, when Mike and Annie were with her, she
hadn't actually noticed any pain.

She had absolutely no feeling below her waist now. As the
dinghy turned with the waves, she had to pull her legs behind
her to adjust to each new position, and it was getting more difficult because they were so numb. She wanted to keep land in
sight, even if it was just a glimpse over her shoulder. The dinghy had deflated even more, and as a result there was slack in
the painter. When the three of them were on the dinghy, it was
taut, but now she had to wind and wind the sloppy portion of
the rope around her wrist. Once in a while, when the wind decreased a little in strength and the swells seemed to steady out
a bit, she attempted to rest her body. She knew it was fruitless
to rest her mind. She had seen too much and felt too much. And
she knew that if she didn't keep repeating the facts, her memory would shatter like her heart.

She checked her watch: two P.M. It was now twelve hours

since the collision. She started with the last position she had charted and went through the events in a detailed timeline. She shouted out every detail. She recited the alphabet to stay alert. She sang Joni Mitchell's "Big Yellow Taxi" to remind her of Ben, her little man, who always made sure that if a song was stuck in his head, it had to be stuck in hers. Just before she had cocooned him in his blanket on his last night, he told her that if a song had to get stuck, this was the one he wanted it to be.

There were jellyfish all around her, washing over her, going up her sleeves, going up her pant legs. They didn't sting, but they didn't leave her alone. A soaring albatross landed by her on the water and then hung around. She wanted to rest, maybe close her eyes and sleep, but whenever she stopped talking aloud or singing or howling with grief, the albatross came closer and pecked at the inflatable tube. Judy couldn't let the huge bird damage the dinghy any further, so she kept repeating the story over and over and the alphabet backward and forward.

She checked her watch: eight P.M. Eighteen hours since the collision. The whole day had gone by without a rescue or a reprieve in the weather. It was wretched to get close enough to make out the shoreline and then to be tossed back by the whim of the currents. She had to tamp down the rising hysteria at the thought of another night in the dinghy.

The second night, there was no moon, no stars. In the utter darkness she took some comfort from following the masthead lights of the sailboats as they headed toward Opua. Each time she saw a boat's navigation lights, she imagined she knew who it was from the check-ins on the Hole in the Net, and she would scream their names.

She forced herself to continue her recitations. She was exceptionally cold; it had been impossible to warm up after those two hours of struggling to get back on top of the dinghy. The cold made her remember a night so long ago with Mike, before they were married. They had sailed up north from Seattle in *Mika*, and they were stuck in an anchorage with howling winds and sheets of rain. She was a southern California girl, and Mike was laughing as he lit the little kerosene heater, saying, "It's summer, Judith!"

Nevertheless, he had made sure the cabin was cozy, and he wrapped her in a blanket. When she warmed up, she took out some wool to resume a knitting project. Mike watched her for a while, and then said, "I'd like to try that. It looks like all those fancy knots I had to learn in the Sea Scouts." Judy told him that she had plenty of yarn but only one pair of knitting needles.

"Never mind, Judith. I'll use pencils," Mike replied.

Somehow he managed to finish his project, a vest for his mother, with pencils rather than knitting needles. When Judy hooted that it wasn't the prettiest of vests, Mike pointed out that his mother would think any gift made by one of her kids was the most beautiful present in the world.

Judy had agreed wholeheartedly. And now the thought of Catherine, her mother-in-law, and her own mother never knowing what had happened to them made her determined to go on.

In the darkness, with no moon, in the middle of the night, she wondered where she was. She had seen no sailboats for several hours, and she couldn't get her bearings. She was exhausted, cold, and desperate. Each time the dinghy got close to land, the sound of breaking waves roared in her ears. She was terrified at the thought of being smashed against the rugged cliffs of the headland she had seen at dusk. She tried to steer herself away from land by furiously paddling with her hands. She knew the dread she felt wasn't unreasonable. Part of it was reflexive; all sailors listen for the sound of breaking waves. Over the years, Judy had seen the smashed results of ships getting too close to rocks or reefs. If large vessels could be reduced to splinters, what would happen to her body?

Earlier, when the three of them were still on top of the dinghy and clinging to the painter, Judy had asked Mike for a kiss. He was despondent at the time, and Judy was surprised at the fervor of his embrace, and at the passion in his kiss. Now she yearned for him. Why should she have to long for Mike? Why should she have to long for her family? Why not join them? Being brutally shattered and destroyed by a sea cliff was not the death she had ever imagined for herself. If she followed Mike's suggestion, submerging herself and holding her breath, it could be a quick death. And she was so tired, God, she was tired. Please forgive me, God, she prayed, but you have shown me the face of death up close and I can't bear it. I really can't bear it.

Despite the mounting panic, Judy knew she had to figure out a way to tell her loved ones the family was never coming back. She recalled that Maureen had often remarked on Judy's unique "heart" ring. The stones were channel-set rather than on prongs, so the ring would probably make it to land intact. The ring would have to be the clue to their demise. She felt in the dark for the stainless steel eyebolt and untied the painter. She took the ring off her finger and slipped the painter through it. When she had worked the ring to about the middle point, she retied the painter as securely as she could. She would push the dinghy toward shore; someday when it was found, somebody would realize that a ring around a painter and an abandoned dinghy were significant. And Maureen, prearranged as her emergency contact, would know that this was Judy's way of saying goodbye; that there was no further reason to conduct a search, no reason for the families to sit by the phone for the next two years, waiting and worrying. She pushed the dinghy on its way and slipped underwater.

"Open your mouth, let out your breath, and take in as much water as possible. Keep doing it so your lungs can fill." She could hear herself repeating Mike's instructions.

She rose up unwillingly. Five more times she tried to drown herself by trapping water in her pants, holding her breath, and going down, but each time she burst to the surface. Her agitation dissolved; this was her family looking after her, helping her to survive, she thought. *They're in heaven now, and they want me to make it to shore to tell our story.*

She thought she must be fairly close to the land; the water was warmer and so was she. As she warmed up, she didn't feel so desperate or afraid, even if it meant going back out to sea to avoid the rocks until morning. And then she remembered that she had sent the dinghy on its telltale mission.

Judy forced herself to remain calm. She lay on her back in the water and rested for a few minutes, and then, most auspiciously, some of the clouds parted and left a sliver of moon and stars. She saw the white bottom of the dinghy, although it was still impossible to tell if it was heading to land or away from it. After hours of swimming, with her lower body useless and the waves still fairly high, she reached the dinghy. The undertaking used up most of the night, but she was finally approaching land.

In daylight, Judy could clearly see the coastline, the high, rocky cliffs that looked forbidding. Better not to think of that. Judy began her recitations again, positioned on the dinghy with her head toward the cliffs. The wind was decreasing and the seas were becoming more settled, and she felt more hopeful. *If I say the alphabet backward and forward sixty times, and if I recite the details of the collision three more times, and if I sing "Big Yellow Taxi,"* she told herself, *I'll see a spotter plane.*

She didn't. She kept singing and praying and reciting, but no one came to rescue her. She checked her watch: two P.M. It was thirty-six hours since the collision. She must have wondered, Is this how I will mark time until the end of my life?

The dinghy brought her in closer to land. The waves were coming in sets, causing her to surf faster and faster toward the dreaded rocks.

"Michael, help me, help me," she kept screaming.

She lay down on the dinghy with her head toward the slightly deflated bow. With each wave, she pulled on the painter as hard as she could to raise the bow and paddled with the other arm to control direction. The waves suddenly picked the dinghy up, and she landed with it on a rocky shelf. At last, high and dry, she thought. Out of that tormenting ocean.

But she was going to have to go back in. The ledge was too uneven, and she was unbalanced. She couldn't take the chance that she would be swept back in without any control over her circumstances or her course. Judy pushed herself to the edge of the precipice, held on firmly to the painter and a pontoon, and waited for the next large surge to wash her back into the sea. When she was back in the water, she slipped off the dinghy, untied the painter from the stainless steel eyebolt, wound it around her wrist, and made her way dog-paddling through the rocky obstacle course. She wasn't dragging the dinghy behind her for sentimental reasons; she had no idea where she was, and she might need it to take her onward.

She sighted a little bay with a small strip of beach, and as she paddled toward it, the strong undercurrent kept pulling her back. She persisted in trying to get to the beach, but the undertow repeatedly threw her onto the rocky bottom. It seemed to take hours, but she finally reached the bank. It was steep, and her hands were all cut up from the rocks. She was done in, thirsty, and confused. Where was she? Who were all these people? She understood that the one near the water's edge was named Nico and that he was the chief, and both he and his wife were watching her carefully as they used their long bamboo poles to fish.

"Can you help me, please? Can I hang on to your bamboo pole?" Judy asked the chief.

"You can do it. Trust me. I promise that you can," Chief Nico replied.

It took her at least two more hours to crawl, digging into the rocky bottom, to the driftwood line, safely away from the breaking waves and the undercurrent, and then, with a last effort, she managed to haul herself and the dinghy up onto the grass.

She couldn't move her hips and legs, but she thought the other people on the beach would come to her aid. "Can you help me, please?" She could hear them chattering and moving about, but as she asked again for assistance, she didn't realize she was completely alone and hallucinating.

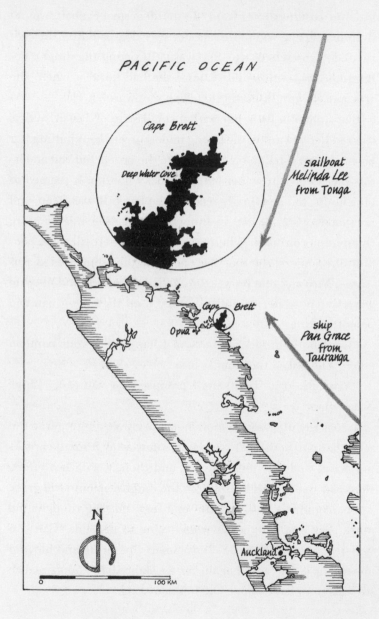

PACIFIC OCEAN

Cape Brett

Deep Water Cove

sailboat
Melinda Lee
from Tonga

Cape Brett

Opua

ship
Pan Grace
from
Tauranga

N

Auckland

0          100 KM

Forty-two hours in the dinghy. Now Judy lay on the grass, dehydrated, depleted, and bleeding. The physical exertion and mental anguish made her overwrought, and she couldn't settle down. It had taken an entire day to reach this cove, and the sun was setting. It was urgent that she get out of her wet clothing before it got too dark and too cold. A part of her mind stayed alert to the tasks still at hand.

Judy struggled to remove her clothing. Her foul-weather pants came off inside out, and she noticed that while they were red on the outside, the inside lining was a bright yellow. This was encouraging; yellow is considered an international color of distress, since yellow and orange are the easiest colors to sight from a distance. She would lay them out in the morning. She took off her fleece jacket and, very systematically, working from the center, wrung out all the water. She took off her black T-shirt, flung it aside, and put the polar fleece layer back on. Next she tried to get the fleece pants off, but it was just too difficult. The only thing she could do was to pull the fabric away from her legs and twist the material to get as much water out as possible. But it wasn't just water; she had shells embedded in her hands and feet, and she was covered with diesel and jellyfish and urine. She collapsed into a dreamless sleep.

In the morning she awoke to the sound of voices, but they were the hallucinations of hope. She saw that she was in a tiny cove. The beach at the shoreline was partly sandy, but mainly rocks. She was lying farther up, on the grass, and behind her were steep hills covered with what appeared to be impenetrable native bush. Over to one side were the tall, green, swordlike flax plants ubiquitous in New Zealand. The Maori and many artists use them to create baskets and bags, and she had read about them in one of her arts books. She wondered if the roots were succulent, and if there were any other plants with cupped leaves holding precious rainwater. She was parched.

Judy crawled toward the flax, but she didn't have the strength to go very far. She couldn't see any other possible water source, critical to her survival. Nearby, though, she discovered sticks scattered about, and found two that were three feet long. She tightened the Velcro on the ankles of the inside-out foul-weather pants and stuck the driftwood sticks into the legs. She had fashioned a perfect hailing distress flag, a big yellow V. Every time a boat went by, she raised her flag and waved and screamed, but no one saw her. She realized she was too low to be observed and would have to move again. She managed to drag herself over to a rock ledge about ten feet away. Although the movement exacerbated her pain, she was somehow able to get herself into a sitting position. All day she sat and waited for boats to pass by, and all day she waved her yellow pants and no-body came. There was a hornets' nest on the rocks nearby, and the hornets swarmed around her face. She knew time was running out. She had never been so thirsty, and she calculated that that she had been without drinking water for at least sixty hours. According to her Medicine at Sea classes, she had twelve more hours.

Another boat came by and she screamed and waved, but there was no response. She looked at her watch. It was just after four P.M.; it would be dark by eight. She was grateful that it was spring in the Southern Hemisphere, with the longer hours of daylight. She saw a dark cloud moving above her and thought, *Thank goodness, it's going to rain and I won't die of dehydration before I get to tell my story*. She took the sticks out of the foul-weather pants and used the pants to form a well in her lap to collect the forthcoming water. The cloud passed by without dropping any water, but as she looked up at it in despair, she noticed there was a plane flying low overhead. She hurried to get the sticks back into the pants so she could wave, but she was too slow. Like the cloud, the plane continued on.

*Eleven*

# Searching for *Melinda Lee*

❋

IN MARCH 1995, WHEN ANNIQUE, HER HUSBAND, MARCO, and their little girl, Geneva, departed from Panama for the Galápagos Islands, they remained in contact with five or six other boats on the same route through their marine radios. The short, informal daily chats about weather and well-being evolved into what they called the Hole in the Net, with a regular schedule and a prescribed format.

From the Galápagos to the Marquesas, there were twenty-five international boats, including the *Melinda Lee*, making the same long passage to French Polynesia. Annique told everyone that she had been designated as net controller because she was bossier than anyone else. In truth, her beautiful English accent was soothing, and according to her listeners, she was always unflustered and methodical. Every boat that joined the net gave Annique background information, including the type, size, and color of boat, number of persons aboard, and a land-based emergency contact phone number. The net gave everyone a sense of community, but they didn't meet in person until they reached the Marquesas, where they celebrated the successful end of a passage with a big potluck dinner on the beach.

It was advantageous that Annique was proficient, because the net grew. They collected boats on passages from the Marquesas to the Tuamotus, Tahiti, the Cook Islands, Niue, Fiji, and several other islands as they continued westward across the South Pacific. Annique and Marco had a special spot in their hearts for *Melinda Lee*. They had first encountered the Sleavins in Colón, Panama, and the two families shared adventures as they continued to cross paths. Their daughter, Geneva, enjoyed playing with Ben and Annie, and when she was four years old, Geneva had her first-ever sleep away from home aboard *Melinda Lee*, in the Cook Islands.

In the Southern Hemisphere's spring season, as boats began to depart from Tonga and Fiji, the Hole in the Net resumed. Those who selected Australia as their destination split off and formed their own net.

Thirty boats were heading to New Zealand over a period of several weeks in November 1995, and the Hole in the Net resumed. Annique conducted roll call every morning and, when weather conditions were especially bad, in the evening as well.

---

Thursday 23 November, 1995

Morning Roll Call

0845–0930 (NZDT) (NZ daylight savings time)

Boat: MELINDA LEE

Location: lat 33°13' S, long 176°24' E

Course: 180 Magnetic, speed 5.5–6.5 knots

Wind: E 25–30 (Gust 37)

Seas: 8'

Cloud cover: 80%

Barometer: 1020 (up 7)

Other: 130 nm (nautical miles) to Opua, staysail only

Note: AQUAVIT (in Opua harbor) makes a contact and they switch frequencies.

(Last transmission from the MELINDA LEE to the Hole in the Net. From the Log of Annique Goldenberg, Net Controller, on the sailing vessel RUQUCA, sailing from Fiji to New Zealand.)

--------------------------------------------------------------------------------

Ten boats on their way to the North Island of New Zealand followed the *Melinda Lee* on the roll call, some going to Opua, some to Whangarei, and some to Auckland. In each report the wind and sea conditions varied slightly, but everyone was concerned about a weather report forecasting two fronts coming in.

--------------------------------------------------------------------------------

Friday 24 November, 1995

Morning Roll Call

0845—0930 (NZDT)

Boat: MELINDA LEE

Note: No check-in. I assume they are busy checking in at Opua.

Log addendum: Since MELINDA LEE is fastidious about maintaining regular contact, I call Kerikeri Radio to ask if Judy had checked in the evening of Thursday, 23 November. Kerikeri Radio says no.

--------------------------------------------------------------------------------

Routinely, Annique urged all boats to check in whenever they made landfall, assuring the net of their safe arrival. Not all did; some were occupied with immigration procedures, and some were asleep after a long passage. If a boat did not respond on roll call, Annique requested information from other boats in the anchorage. On this particular passage, many boats also checked in with Kerikeri Radio, an official station in the Bay of Islands with weather information.

---

Friday 24 November 1995

Morning Roll Call

1800 (NZDT)

Log addendum: AQUAVIT (in Opua) tells me that MELINDA LEE has still not arrived in Opua; they have been waiting for them. AQUAVIT's VHF is not good and so they asked WALACHIN to check on VHF to see if anyone else has seen them. No one has.

I call Kerikeri on 4445.0 KHz after evening roll call to ask if they have heard from ML tonight (24th), they have had no contact tonight but we are told that ML checked in last night after all. They passed on the message that they have battery problems and will be in on Sat. (25th) morning. Great relief.

---

---

Saturday 25 November 1995

0830–0930 (NZDT)

Boat: MELINDA LEE

Note: THEY HAVE NOT ARRIVED IN OPUA.

Log addendum:

AQUAVIT informed us that there was confusion at Kerikeri. The vessel with battery problems due to arrive Sat. morning is MARY LOU TOO.

MELINDA LEE HAS STILL NOT ARRIVED.

Kerry on MYTHRA and Lewjean on WINDOW are 100% sure that MELINDA LEE did check in with KERIKERI the evening roll call of Thursday 23rd Nov.

They remember that MELINDA LEE (JUDY) said they would arrive the following morning (FRIDAY 24th) in Opua, no position given.

Word will go out on the various nets to look out for MELINDA LEE.

NOTE: After the net I speak to Kerikeri to inform them that we have not had any word from MELINDA LEE on our net this morning (25th).

Have they heard anything? No.

I also inform them that 2 of the boats on my net clearly remember MELINDA LEE checking in with Kerikeri the evening roll call of Thurs. 23rd Nov. Kerikeri will check their log book as soon as they can.

I give them the last known information I have on MELINDA LEE from the morning of Thurs. 23rd Nov. Plus any information I have on the boat:

(Info given): MIKE, JUDY, BEN (9) ANNIE (7) SLEAVIN * USA * WCQ 7351 * 47' COMPASS CUTTER * WHITE HULL / BLUE STRIPE / BLUE DECK * 406 EPIRB * 6-PERSON GOODYEAR LIFE-RAFT *

I also inform them that MELINDA LEE was very good about checking in every day. In my opinion they have some problem as they have missed two check-ins and they are definitely overdue.

[We believe] THEY LOST CONTACT BETWEEN THE HOURS OF 1930 ON THE 23rd AND 0830 ON THE 24th.

RUQUCA arrives in Opua in the afternoon (Saturday 25th).

I have various conversations with Kerikeri on the VHF.

I pass on a contact address in the USA we have for MELINDA LEE:

Maureen (Reenie) Lull and her address and phone number in Hermosa Beach, California.

AQUAVIT has been very active in alerting people to the fact that MELINDA LEE is DEFINITELY OVERDUE AND HAS CEASED RADIO CONTACT.

---

---

Sunday 26 November 1995

Morning Net

0845–0930 (NZDT)

Log Addendum: NO WORD FROM MELINDA LEE.

NO SIGHTINGS FROM OTHER YACHTS ON THE NET.

YACHTS STILL OUT THERE CONTINUE TO KEEP A LOOK OUT.

WE ARE INFORMED BY KERIKERI THAT THE SEARCH HAS BEEN CLASSIFIED CLASS 3, WHICH IS WHEN THE VESSEL MIGHT BE 30 OR MORE MILES OFFSHORE. IT REQUIRES AN AIRCRAFT THAT HAS LONGER RANGE THAN ONE SEARCHING THE COASTLINE. AN ORION WILL BE FLYING THIS MORNING TO SEARCH, PLUS ANY SMALL AIRCRAFT IN THE DISTRICT.

---

Early that afternoon, Sunday, November 26, at Kerikeri Radio's request, Annique and Marco invited other sailors to come aboard *Ruquca* to gather information. They tried to plot *Melinda Lee*'s course, discussed the possibility of equipment malfunctions, and took collective notes on any ship sightings.

All of this information was given to Jon and Maureen Cullen, the operators of Kerikeri Radio. It was conveyed to search and rescue personnel, who were also told the net had been in regular contact over the passage, *Melinda Lee* was always meticulous about responding during a passage and upon arrival, and contact had ceased suddenly. They were also informed of the last possible position of the *Melinda Lee,* as deduced by the cooperative effort of several yachts from the net.

The National Rescue Coordination Centre (NRCC) in Wellington, the capital of New Zealand, had charge of the search. Since they were looking for a vessel some thirty miles offshore, the search was designated a Class 3, and a Royal New Zealand Air Force Orion aircraft with the necessary range would be sent out to sea. The officials plotted out their search patterns, with an initial investigative area of 144 square miles. The Orion would be sent out to sea, and the NRCC recommended that the Northland Search and Rescue Squad conduct a coastline search. The positions on this squad are voluntary; all the members also hold full-time jobs with the Whangarei police force.

Sergeant Dave Palmer was very experienced in the field of search and rescue when he was assigned as officer in charge of the mission to look for *Melinda Lee* on the afternoon of Sunday, November 26. He had participated in many rescue and recovery efforts, both land- and sea-based. Since the Northland area has two thousand miles of coastline and a significant number of recreational vessels, 80 percent of search-and-rescue missions are marine related. In fact, Sergeant Palmer had completed extensive training exercises in the exact area to which he was now being sent. He was to cover the Northland coast in a Cessna four-seater plane flying from Bream Head, the Whangarei Harbor entrance, to the Cavalli Islands, north of the Bay of Islands. He would be accompanied by another member of the police force, Constable Renee Orbon, and the pilot.

Sergeant Palmer had to take the weather conditions into account and work out the drift and leeway factors for wind and current. There had been two days of strong northeasterly winds since the last known contact with the yacht; in that case, he concluded, there was a strong chance the yacht had been blown into Cape Brett, and they would be looking for debris and bodies.

They flew up the coastline from Whangarei, and after forty minutes rounded Cape Brett. It was an uncomfortable flight in a light airplane, with northeast winds still blowing 30 to 40 knots. They flew across Deep Water Cove, and from a distance Sergeant Palmer observed a small white craft on the beach. The turbulence prevented the pilot from flying lower to get a closer look, but Sergeant Palmer noted that there appeared to be two or three people near the boat, and none in distress, so the Cessna continued on. Sergeant Palmer recalled almost immediately that he might have seen another person up from the boat, lying on the ground and not moving. He commented to the pilot that they weren't too far off track, and he would like to go back for a closer look. As they circled, he could see that the person lying down was still not moving but was now waving something yellow, that the white craft was an inflatable, and that the two people near it were sitting quietly on the bank. Gusty winds buffeted the plane, and an overhead power cable that went from Deep Water Cove to the lighthouse at Cape Brett made it impossible to get any closer. The pilot of the Cessna dipped his wing as he circled, a sign to assure the person waving that he or she was seen. There was a marine radio on the plane, and Sergeant Palmer put out a call for any boats nearby to come into Deep Water Cove to assist.

Sid Hepi and his uncle, Steve Willoughby, were fishing from the family runabout, *Salt Shaker*, in a protected bay not too far from Deep Water Cove when they heard the call for assistance on their radio. They heard the captain of *Tiger Lily 3*, a Fuller's tour boat, respond to the spotter plane and ask for information. They listened as the *Tiger Lily*'s captain was told there was a sighting of an overturned inflatable in Little Hauai Bay that required investigation. Sid knew the topography of the bay and Deep Water Cove well; he had once worked there for the New Zealand Department of Conservation. Sid and Steve decided to go over to see if they could help. As they approached, they saw that the tour boat couldn't get into the cove at all because a large swell was running through the little bay. Steve got the aluminum boat in as close as he could to the rocky shore, but it was very rough and he was unable to land. Steve stayed with the boat while Sid jumped out and waded through the water. He made his way through the rocks, up the grass, and over to the ledge where Judy sat, not moving. He sat down beside her and quietly told her his name. She started crying when she saw him. She tried to give him a few details about herself and the family, including her name and the name *Melinda Lee,* but he couldn't understand her very well.

"Are you okay?" he asked.

"I'm so thirsty, do you think you could get me some water?" she mumbled. She was quite incoherent, and Sid had to ask her to repeat herself. It hurt when she talked. Her lips were so cracked and swollen, and the skin felt stretched and raw.

Sid went back to the *Salt Shaker* to retrieve the water bottle and informed Steve Willoughby of the details he had gathered, including Judy's name. Steve relayed the information to Sergeant Dave Palmer in the Cessna, and when asked how Judy was, Steve responded, "Absolutely gutted."

This was the first sighting of anyone from the overdue yacht. Only one person was in fact present in the bay, and Sergeant Palmer blamed eyestrain for his report of the two additional people. They called in the find to Inspector John Meads, the New Zealand Police rescue coordinator, who arranged with the Northland Emergency Services Trust to send a helicopter.

Sid returned to Judy and gave her some water. She asked for more, but he was cautious because she looked so weak and dehydrated. He just didn't know if it would be good for her to have too much. He reassured her that she was safe and that he would stay with her. He gave her small sips of water, and once she felt more comfortable, she started telling Sid what had happened to her and her family. Her speech was still quite garbled, and the story itself seemed incomprehensible to him. Sid thought she must be confused, but he was very upset by the story and very concerned for her, especially as he could tell "she was a foreigner and would feel very alone."

Sid Hepi is related to everyone in nearby Rawhiti. The *Salt*

*Shaker* was technically owned by Steve Willoughby's brother Robert, Sid's uncle, but everyone in Rawhiti considered it a family boat; it was used to ferry those who worked at the Otehei Bay Arts and Craft Centre on Urapukapuka Island, where Steve Willoughby was the manager. Sid and Steve had ferried Lara, Sid's wife, to Urapukapuka that morning, and they were to pick her up at four P.M. when her shift ended. It was past that now, but Sid and Steve would not leave Judy before the helicopter arrived. They felt responsible for her and knew that Lara would completely understand. Indeed, the *Salt Shaker* would later be used by two other cousins to comb the shoreline up and down for hours and kilometers, searching for the bodies of Judy's loved ones. They hoped to give her the opportunity to say good-bye in a proper and ceremonial way.

Steve Simpson and Reg Ellwood, the helicopter pilots from the community-funded Northland Emergency Services Trust, didn't initially know this would be a land-based rescue. They had with them a paramedic and a water-rescue crew member who was prepared to drop by rope ladder into the sea and assist four people in a disabled yacht. As they approached Deep Water Cove, they saw rocks everywhere, making it too difficult to land. "Man, we're going to catch the blades," Steve recalls saying. He called Steve Willoughby on the marine radio and asked him if they could take Judy on the *Salt Shaker* to another bay, where the helicopter could land and meet her. Steve Willoughby readily agreed. Sid asked Judy if she thought she could get along to their boat with his assistance.

"I think I broke my back and my neck. I can't move at all," Judy whispered. She seemed to be in extreme agony.

Once he learned there was no other option, Steve Simpson managed to guide the helicopter toward the flax and land. When all four of the helicopter team, in their big, puffy, orange survival suits, got out and ran over to Judy, she said, "Are you from Ghostbusters?"

The paramedic did a thorough examination. He determined that Judy had broken her back, sustained a severe blow to her head, and was very dehydrated, but he told her that none of her injuries were fatal. The pilots wanted to look for the rest of the family. They put her on a stretcher, got her strapped safely in the helicopter, and told her of their plans. They assured her that they would keep her as comfortable as possible, but they wanted the opportunity to do a search while there was still daylight.

"It's no use," she sobbed, "they're all dead."

"You can't be sure," Steve replied. "Perhaps you just lost sight of them."

"I'm sure. I'll tell you why I'm so sure," Judy mumbled. "I saw them die. . . ."

The search-and-rescue team was dubious. Judy had been hallucinating as a result of her dehydration. Judy had been barely coherent. But their presence seemed to give her some kind of ethereal resolve, and she shook her head emphatically.

"My family is dead!" she cried.

And then she told them the story she had stayed alive to tell during those terrible hours. For thirty minutes, starting with the position of collision and Ben's death, she told them everything. The four men were completely mesmerized. She told it with such clarity that Steve Simpson can repeat every detail even today.

-------------------------------------------------------------------------------------

Sunday 26 November, 1995

1630 (NZDT)

Log Addendum:

WE HEARD A PLANE HAD SPOTTED AN OVERTURNED VESSEL IN DEEPWATER COVE. WE SUBSEQUENTLY DIS-COVERED THAT IT WAS JUDY AND THAT SHE IS BEING FLOWN TO WHANGAREI HOSPITAL.

-------------------------------------------------------------------------------------

# Twelve

# The Moan of Condolences

❋

MAUREEN LULL WAS ECSTATIC. SHE WAS QUITE SURE
she was pregnant and was impatient to confirm it at her physician's office. Maureen had been the first one to offer to have a
baby shower for Judy before Annie's birth, and she couldn't
wait to have her own child. She was in a wonderful mood. Then
the phone rang, and the caller identified himself as a member of the Whangarei, New Zealand, police force. At first she
thought it was Judy making a prank call.

"Is this Maureen Lull?" the caller repeated. "You have been
identified as the emergency contact for Michael and Judith
Sleavin."

Maureen and Richard Lull had spent two weeks on *Melinda
Lee* in the Dominican Republic. It had been such a great
time, even though it was the beginning of what Judy called
the "move fast" period. They visited a number of anchorages

on the north coast, which gave Richard and Maureen the opportunity to learn the night watch routine. Each night, the four adults took advantage of the calmer winds from dusk until dawn to sail to the next bay. The Lulls owned a sailboat, a Shock 35, *Aftershock*, and both were experienced ocean racers. On the southern California coast, there was nowhere to race but offshore. They, too, were contemplating a future cruising life, and the two-week trip on the *Melinda Lee* provided a real education.

Maureen, always a supremely capable and calm individual, felt her stomach churning as she listened to the voice on the phone. It was inconceivable to her that this could happen to the Sleavins, and now, as the emergency contact, she had the distressing task of having to break the news to their families.

Catherine, Mike's mother, had sailed with the Sleavins on three separate occasions, and she was familiar with life aboard the *Melinda Lee*. In the only interview she gave, to the *Los Angeles Times*, she said, "The children were the most important things in their life. My Michael always thought he was in heaven just to have his children with him twenty-four hours a day."

From the outset, Catherine's honesty and concern for Judy set the tone for her other children. They were all suffering. Mike was incredibly popular and loved in that family. They talked about who would go to New Zealand and what else might be done. John, the youngest, was trying to find out exactly what had happened, and he wanted to make sure there would be an investigation.

Letters from the cruising community poured in as the news spread. Many of the letters were posted from faraway ports. Those who had photos of any of the Sleavins, especially of the children, made the effort to develop and send them to Judy. The family on *SeaHawk* wrote from Pago Pago that they had notified Ben's teacher at the Calvert School. Someone sent Judy a piece of artwork that Annie had done. And another person sent a baseball cap that Ben had worn and passed on to her son. Everyone was concerned that all the tangible remembrances of the family had gone down with the *Melinda Lee*.

Letters arrived from all over the world from people who would never think of stepping onto a boat—empathetic and humane strangers who were touched by Judy's loss and simply wanted to reach out. One man from Singapore sent a kind-hearted letter of support, telling Judy that his wife had died ten years ago, in a terrible accident, after only twenty days of marriage. He said the grief had almost killed him, but he was indeed happy now, a state he once thought impossible. He enclosed one hundred dollars. An English widow of some forty years' duration sent a tender note with eight dollars, and her apologies: she was on a pension. Isabel Allende, the much-admired author, sent a handmade card with three white birds flying high on the cover, in memory of Mike, Ben, and Annie, she said. It was a warm and beautiful card from a woman still and always in pain from the loss of her daughter, Paula, about whom she wrote a book.

Letters came from across New Zealand offering sympathy and more. A flower arrangement from a couple in Remuera, Auckland, arrived with these sentiments: "My dear lady, if it were possible to erase the last few days for you indeed we would. We offer you support in any way you may require, please don't hesitate to call us, collect, and know that our home is open to you or any extended family members or friends you may be expecting. God bless you."

Meanwhile, I knew none of this. I was in Chicago, taking the examinations required to become a board-certified oral and maxillofacial radiologist. During a break, I bumped into Dr. Lars Hollender, my mentor. I expected him to ask how it was going, but instead he told me he had been watching a story on CNN about a sailing family that was hit—I interrupted him. I always enjoyed talking with Lars, a man of considerable wit and intelligence, but I was fatigued and still had one more full day of exams to go.

Two evenings later, at dinner, another colleague introduced the same topic. "Lucky that you and your husband completed your sailing adventure," he said, as he told me about a story he had read in the *Los Angeles Times*. At first I listened with the detached interest of someone well acquainted with that same rough passage, but who would never actually know sailors to whom this could happen. But Stu was a detail man, and he mentioned the children's ages and the fact that the mother, who had survived, was a civil engineer. He didn't recall their names, or wouldn't tell me, when he saw the look of dread on my face as the story finally sank in.

I rushed back to the hotel to call my husband, John.

"Are you keeping something from me?" I asked. I was so afraid of what he was going to say.

"Oh, honey, I'm so sorry, I didn't know what to do," he replied. "This last year has been so grueling with your preparation, and I felt that I shouldn't interfere with the Boards." He told me Mike's brother had called, and he read me the notes he had taken, but absolutely nothing made sense. I lay down on the bed and wept.

I remembered Ben's first birthday. John and I were staying with the Sleavins at their home in Saugus, California. Judy came and sat beside me and told me Ben's godmother was her oldest and dearest friend, Bonnie, whom she had met in Ohio during her restaurant years.

"Mike and I would be honored if you will be the godmother of our next child. Whether it's a boy or a girl, we want our next one to be just like you!"

"A crazy cruiser on a small boat, you mean?" I asked.

"No, a person just like you, in all respects," she said.

"Are you pregnant now?" I asked.

"No, but we're madly working on it," she said.

"But I'll be out at sea. How can I possibly be a good and responsible godmother?"

"You have your ways." Judy said.

I cried, and hugged Mike and Judy and said, "Yes, of course, thank you, thank you, I am so honored to be chosen."

In October 1988, on a passage between Tonga and Fiji, John and I had our trusty ham radio operator Russ Faudre relay a phone patch to the Sleavins in Saugus.

"You have a beautiful little goddaughter, Anna Rose Sleavin, born October second. Over."

"I can't wait to meet her. Tell her I love her. Over."

I loved being Annie's godmother. When she was not yet four, we went to Disneyland together. She held my hand on every ride and whispered to me not to be scared in the darkness of the Pirates of the Caribbean experience.

When we were on the *Melinda Lee* sailing with the family to Costa Rica, she once fell and lay with her head in my lap as I treated the large cut over her eye.

"You're very brave," I told her.

"Okay, but tell me the story again about Trixie," she said. She loved stories about my girlhood cocker spaniel.

She often climbed up on my lap, and because of the extreme heat, we'd be stuck together, bare legs against bare legs. It was heaven for me.

And Ben. He was funny.

"I know the exact song to teach other kids who don't know any English," he told me. 'Do Wah Diddy'!"

His uncle Jeremy Graves would later say as part of his eulogy, "Since my son is the same age as Ben, I always had a measuring stick by which I could gauge what Ben was learning. When we visited the *Melinda Lee*, I saw that Ben's world had expanded in so many new directions by meeting new people, seeing new lands, eating new foods, hearing new languages, hearing new music. When he was seven years old, he showed my son Austin and me how to set a course, hold the wheel, and read the compass. The world he was growing up in truly amazed me."

It was fortunate that so many members of the family had come to visit the Sleavins on the *Melinda Lee* in various ports in the

Caribbean, to have the opportunity to share, as one of them put it, the fantastic quality of their lives. The younger generation—the cousins Sara, Austin, Simon, Drew, and Shannon—would always be enriched by the treasured time they had spent on the *Melinda Lee,* even if they could not begin to comprehend its ending.

The *Melinda Lee* was always ready for company. An excerpt from one of the group letters we had all received:

*Come visit, you won't go home hungry. Seriously, let Maureen know if you'd like to come visit, we have lots of open dates (like from now to eternity).*

—Love, the Sleavins

*Thirteen*

# The Sailboat

✦

MIKE'S FAMILY GOT TOGETHER AND DECIDED THAT Colleen Polley, Mike's sister, would go to New Zealand immediately. Two of her children, Drew and Shannon, were almost the same ages as Ben and Annie. Shannon and Annie were only six weeks apart in age. The two girls had made many plans while the Polleys were visiting in the Virgin Islands. Annie said having a cousin was even better than having a friend. They had giggled madly at the idea of sailing to a place called The Baths because the water was as warm as a tub.

As her flight took off, Colleen wondered how her husband, Jerry, was going to be able to tell Drew and Shannon what had happened to their adored relatives. And, she wondered, what would Shannon, at her tender age, even understand?

At age seven, Shannon Polley wrote the following:

# Sailboat

Once I went on this realy **fun** trip. It was on my aunts and uncles sail boat. They were trying to sail around the world. My aunt's name was Judy and my uncle's name is Mike. My aunt and uncle had two kids. A son and a daghter. The son's name is Ben and the daghter's name is Annie. The son is abant my brothers age and the daghter is abant my age. Annie and Ben are my favorite cosins. Mike and Judy where my favorite uncle and aunt too. Relatives Relatives would come and visit them on the sail boat sailboat. One time we decided to go visit them on there sailboat. My dad couldn't go because he had to work. So it was just my mom, my brother, and me. My mom was pregnat with my little sister but we didn't know it then. It was a long and hard trip to get there.

When we finally got there I fell down alot. I didn't have good sea legs. When I finally got my sea legs I started to explore. It was a pretty big sailboat. Finally we started up the ingin and were on are way. We visited alot of places. My favorite was the

Baths. It was called that because the water was so __warm__. The Baths was a island. After we had swam around the island for a wile, we started to explore on land. There was a special trail that you had to hike in your bathing suit because it was so wet. There were rope latters to clime, caves to go through, and little places were you could stop and swim. Practicly the whole hike you were walking in __warm__ water.

Finally the trip had to end. I missed my dad but I still wanted to stay on the saiboat longer. I seid goodbye to my cosine, aunt, and uncle. I was on my way home. When we got back home we saw a sine on the house that seid "WELCOME HOME!!". I was glad to see my my dad. I gave my dad the presents I boght him and the went outside to play with the welcom home gifts my dad boght me. One day my dad came and told me and my brother some tarable news. My dad seid my aunts and uncles boat had sunk. A much larger boat had hit my uncles an aunts boat.

It was so big that it didn't even notice wen it hit my aunts and uncles boat. It was at night time and every one was asleep. Mike, Judy, and Annie exaped. My cousin Ben sleped rite through it. My uncle went under the water to se if he could save Ben. He never came back up. My aunt managed to cime on the life raft. My cousin Annie just kind of disipeared. My aunt Judy was the only surviver. She wash up on a desserted island. Judy ate some grass to keep from starving. The grass made her sick. Many days later some people fond her. They took her to the hospitil. She was skraped, bruzed, had a hurt back, and was being treated for some other things. But she liked. She is still my favorite aunt.

The end

*Fourteen*

# Willing to Live

✦

AFTER A TWENTY-MINUTE RIDE, THE HELICOPTER TRANS-
porting Judy landed on the roof of the Whangarei Hospital,
the main hospital in the Northland District. Judy, wrapped in
a silver hypothermia blanket, was carried on a gurney to the
emergency room. Straightaway, she asked the nurse for water,
but was told they would have to check things out first.

"Check things out? I thought you were taking me to a party,
all wrapped in this silvery paper."

Judy had learned early in life to deflect serious problems
with humor and laughter, an attitude that sometimes seemed
inappropriate to people outside the immediate family. The nurse
was confused by this performance, but Judy felt a little better.
She might still be bleeding from her head wound, but at least
some of her personality was oozing out and attempting to connect with people despite the pervasive sorrow.

She looked damaged, like a package that had been thrown
about. She had bruises over most of her body, and a black eye.

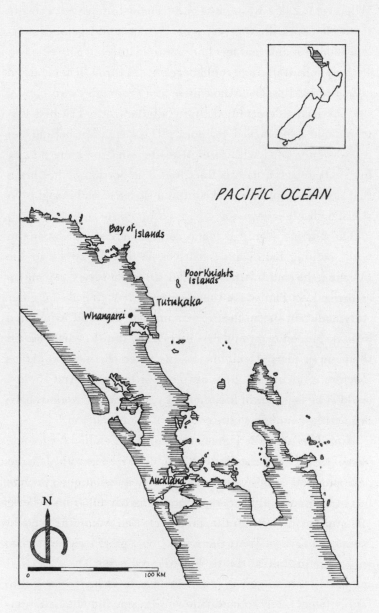

PACIFIC OCEAN

Bay of Islands

Poor Knights Islands

Tutukaka

Whangarei

Auckland

N

0                    100 KM

Wherever her face wasn't raw and reddened from overexposure to the elements, she was very pale. Her feet and legs were swollen, and her hands and feet had multiple infected cuts. She was severely dehydrated and could barely speak through her cracked and blistered lips. Over the course of a thorough examination, the physicians determined that Judy had three crushed vertebrae and two cracked vertebrae. The laceration behind her ear was embedded with foreign matter, and the bony part of her skull in that area was fractured. The portion of her brain that sustained injury would compromise her visual recognition skills, probably irreversibly.

The physician on call made certain Judy slept that night, with soothing balms and sedatives. When she awoke in the morning, she couldn't move and lay still on her back, staring up at the ceiling. She wished now that she had passed along her story and then succumbed to her injuries. She and Annie had been so sure they would be rescued. If the ship had picked them up or alerted authorities, the three of them would be together, grieving for Ben, but at least together. And if they couldn't be together in life, then why couldn't her wounds have been critical enough so she could join them in death?

After Judy's terrified understanding that Ben had died, some part of her had separated into a machine on automatic drive, to deal with Mike and Annie's survival. To a casual observer, she might have seemed heartless, restraining herself from making any attempt, however futile, to look for Ben, but nothing could have been further from the truth. Even grief-stricken to her core, she functioned as the experienced sailor she was, well prepared for emergencies. She was a wife and mother with a family to get safely to land. She was broken, but she had discipline to spare. And she was never one to waste energy trying to undo what already was done. She was someone who moved on to the next step. When Annie, and then Mike, died, she was relieved that the lower half of her body was numb. She was relieved that her head was matted with blood. To her it meant that her injuries were life-threatening and she could die as soon as she told her story. Now she was terrified that she was going to live, without her beloved family.

All the rituals that might have comforted Judy had to go on in her absence. She was immobile, in shock, not ready to respond to the embrace of these familiar rites. While the family was memorialized—at the Church of Saint Patrick in Tacoma; at Temple Beth Haverim in Agoura Hills, California; and at a nondenominational service at the Opua Cruising Club in New Zealand—Judy lay sedated, awaiting her release from the nightmare.

Isabelle was one of the health social workers at Whangarei Hospital. She had finished her usual early-morning swim session and was back in her car, on her way to breakfast at Caffeine Espresso Café, her favorite gathering spot, before heading to work. She was listening to the radio, a story about the sole survivor of a boating tragedy having been airlifted to the hospital the previous night. When she arrived on the ward, Isabelle was immediately assigned to Judy's case, and her first impression of Judy was of someone who had suffered long weather exposure, severe dehydration, and general trauma. But, she observed, the trauma could certainly not be limited to the physical injuries, because no physical pain could account for the torment her eyes held. Although the social workers had training in post-traumatic stress disorder, patients who required their expertise usually had been involved in more conventional incidents. The team assigned to Judy would need more than educational skills. Fortunately, the hospital, and Whangarei itself, would extend to Judy all the attention and consideration she required.

Whangarei is a pleasant little city of about fifty thousand people, less than three hours north of Auckland by car. It is situated on the western end, at the inner reaches of Whangarei Harbor, on the banks of the Hatea River, and is the industrial and commercial center for the Northland. There is an oil refinery, essential to the entire country, at Marsden Point, on the southern side of the harbor entrance. Restaurants and galleries in the Town Basin overlook the international yachts that berth in the city marina. The city itself offers many diverse activities, including nature walks, artists' centers, bookstores, and boutiques. Car repair places, called "panel beater" shops, and marine services are just a walk away from the galleries. Within easy driving distance are beautiful parks and beaches, and as you head out of town in any direction there are rolling hills with dairy farms and orchards. The name Whangarei is Maori in origin and has several meanings; *wh* is pronounced as *f,* and it doesn't hurt to roll the *r* to reveal your cultural interest. In New Zealand, both English and Maori are the official languages.

Colleen, Mike's sister, arrived in Whangarei only twenty-four hours after Judy's admittance. Isabelle offered her a sleeping room at the hospital, but she refused. She slept in a chair by Judy's bed for two and a half weeks. During her entire stay, each time Judy turned her head to look at Colleen, she didn't know who she was.

"Hi, I'm Judy. And you are . . . ?"

Colleen would remind Judy of their relationship, and of the brain injury that caused this loss of recognition. It was so odd and troubling to Judy, this brain injury. She hadn't recognized anyone who came into her hospital room, but of course up to that point they had all been strangers. She could remember with great acuity everything that had happened at sea. She could remember everything about Colleen; she just didn't recognize her from one minute to the next. Colleen didn't mind the repetitions, but this deficit in her brain, termed visual agnosia, was of great concern to Judy, despite the doctor's counsel. In an effort to make some sense of things, she would splatter Colleen with questions.

"Did you cut your hair? Did you change your outfit?"

And each morning when Judy opened her eyes, she didn't recognize the room she was in.

"Did they change the wallpaper?" she asked frequently.

Colleen rarely left the ward. The team assigned to Judy warmed up to her immediately and offered any assistance she might need. On her day off, Isabelle drove Colleen to the Bay of Islands, to an area in the vicinity of the search and rescue. Colleen was very grateful to Isabelle, but it is not unusual for many of the hospital staff in Whangarei to provide outreach care far beyond the physical needs of the patient. Overseas patients and their families are entertained, taken home for dinners, and accompanied on outings.

The Whangarei Hospital staff might be ready for almost anything, but they were completely unprepared for the onslaught of local and international media interested in the Sleavin story. They were shocked to find some of the reporters and photographers on the ward, disguised as cruising friends or as visitors to other patients. There had never been a need to monitor visitors, but it didn't take long for the hospital director to become very protective. Isabelle, too, guarded Judy's privacy fiercely, as she continued to coordinate all the services Judy required. Surgery was scheduled to remove the embedded stones and shells in Judy's feet, a psychiatrist was assigned, and a brace was made for Judy's back. They were anxious for the day when Judy would be more mobile, so they could move her to a side room with increased security.

Isabelle had become accustomed to seeing certain visitors, such as cruising friends Marco and Annique from *Ruquca*, and Martha from *Chandelle*. Still, she was suspicious of every stranger, so when a beautiful woman with a warm, open smile arrived on the ward and inquired after "the American lady," Isabelle adopted her recently acquired, most official manner.

"And just what umbrella are you under?" Isabelle remembers asking her.

"Umbrella? I'm just me," she replied, "and I was wondering if there is anything the American lady needs."

Her gentleness disarmed Isabelle, and the woman, who introduced herself as Diana Moratti, was given a list of items to purchase. Diana, or Babe as she is generally known, went downtown and returned with the purchases: knickers, a dressing gown, and slippers. Only a morsel of American culture had seeped into Whangarei, in the form of a McDonald's, and Babe made a side trip there to buy some "pikelets," as Judy would learn to call pancakes. Babe asked Isabelle what else the American lady might require, and Isabelle told her that eventually she would need accommodation.

"That's no problem, she can live with us," Babe said. "Oh, by the way," she added kindly, "may I know her name?"

Judy's mother, Caryl, came to New Zealand to relieve Colleen at Judy's bedside. She stayed at the hospital, in one of the sleeping rooms offered by Isabelle. Caryl began making arrangements to take Judy to a hotel upon her discharge, and then to a hospital in California when she could travel. Judy remained resolute in her desire to remain in New Zealand. She understood her mother's good intentions, but she was unprepared to call California home without her family, at least in her present condition.

Isabelle told them there were nine offers of accommodation in private homes, and that several in the surrounding area would be screened for appropriateness. Isabelle asked the hospital's occupational therapist to check out Babe and Ian Moratti's place in Tutukaka first. She pronounced it safe and more than manageable for Judy. There was a long driveway with a locked gate for privacy. There were beautiful grounds and a lovely home, with the cottage just steps away. The cottage itself had a bedroom, a tiny kitchen, a tinier bathroom, and a small lounge area where a cot could be placed for any visitors, or, as Judy preferred to call us later, her "adult supervisors."

The drive from Whangarei to Tutukaka took forty-five minutes. When Judy and Caryl arrived, Babe spent the day helping Judy get familiarized with her new home. It didn't take long to put things away; Judy's possessions were limited to the clothing charitably provided by Babe and some cruising friends. When Ian arrived home from work that first night, Judy went down the driveway to meet him at the gate, a walk close to one-third of a mile. Looking back, Judy recalls that there was no sense that they were complete strangers, and she went over and put her arms around him and said, "You must be Ian. Thanks for having me."

He returned the hug and said, "You must be Judy."

And that was that.

Over the years, Babe and Ian have insisted that anyone would have taken Judy in to live with them.

"But she was a total stranger, ruthlessly traumatized," I recently said to Ian.

"So?" he replied.

"Once she left the safe cocoon of the hospital and realized the significance of her loss, anything could have happened," I pressed. "Your property is gorgeous, but your home sits on high cliffs. Judy could have easily thrown herself over."

"We both wanted her to come," Babe said. She was emphatic.

"Aside from the possibility of severe depression," I added, "she had physical injuries to contend with, a constant string of visitors—"

Ian interrupted. "We decided to deal with whatever came up."

"Who wouldn't have done it for her?" they both repeated.

In reality it was an astounding responsibility, but fortunately for Judy, Babe has a gentle and thoughtful nature, and Ian has incredibly good sense. He was born on the North Island and knew what he wanted from life when he finished high school. He flew to Canada with only the money he would need to buy a chainsaw and a few nights' accommodation when he reached British Columbia. He became a lumberjack at Whistler Mountain when there were more trees than ski cabins, and socked away a lot of his earnings in order to buy land, in both British Columbia and New Zealand. When he returned to the North

Island, his friends tried unsuccessfully to talk him out of a purchase in Tutukaka, a small coastal fishing village. The inaccessibility didn't deter him, and he used the rural logging roads to haul up everything he needed to build his home on the magnificent property he bought. He built a small cottage to live in during the building process, and it was this cottage, twenty years later, that Judy would call home, on and off, for the next two and a half years.

*Whangarei, New Zealand*

*Dear Friends and Family,*

*I want to thank everyone for all their love and prayers. It's very comforting to be surrounded by my friends and family, even though we're miles apart.*

*I was discharged from the hospital on December 22, 1995, after 3½ weeks. I went from totally immobile to a walker and then walking with the aid of crutches. As I was walking "laps" down the hospital corridor, I overheard a nurse say, "There goes Judith, taking her crutches for a walk," so I put them down and realized I really didn't need them anymore. It felt good to be walking without any of this hospital equipment, as there were moments when I wondered if and when that would ever happen.*

*I'm now living north of Whangarei, in Tutukaka, in a cottage overlooking the rugged coast. It's beautiful, safe, comfortable and very relaxing. I love it here. I've been doing a lot of walking up and down hills, and can do about three miles a day. It feels great to exercise and get my strength back. I have to wear a corset brace for a total of*

*three months because of the healing of the two crushed
vertebrae. I've also started swimming laps at the Whangarei indoor pool. I wear a float around my waist to keep me
from bending or twisting my back. I'm only at two laps, but
can see that this is a great way to exercise those muscles that
walking doesn't affect.*

*When my sister and niece visited, we went to Auckland
for additional medical appointments. A second opinion on
my back was very positive. A neurologist checked me out,
and I had an MRI. I passed all the tests with flying colors
except for the visual recognition part. The neurologist opened
an International Time Magazine and asked me to identify
three photos. I did not know who they were. They now will
allow me to stay in this country because I couldn't recognize Bill Clinton, O. J. Simpson, and Princess Di.*

*For me, getting my physical strength back and my bones
mended is my first priority. New Zealand is perfect for that.
The medical care here is excellent, and I'm being looked
after daily by a team consisting of doctors, nurses, psychiatrists, social workers, and hydrotherapists.*

*Some days are good, some days are hard, and I know I
have a long bumpy road ahead of me. Your thoughts and
prayers make this horrible tragedy easier to bear. Thank
you again.*

*Love, Judy*

This was the public face of a private mourner. This was the
voice of a proud woman who wanted to show off her successes,
who wanted to reassure her family that she had retained her
sense of humor, and who wouldn't bore anyone with more than

"some days are hard." She mentioned in her letter that doing laps at the Whangarei Aquatic Centre was great exercise, but only Isabelle knew how punishing the decision was for Judy to get back in the water, even into an indoor pool. Only Isabelle was in the dressing room as Judy wept while trying on bathing suits.

Certainly, at the time Judy wrote her reassuring letter, most of her needs were fundamental in nature, but every simple task was overshadowed with the question, why bother?

When Judy's mother left, her sister Risa and her niece arrived. Her mother desperately wanted Judy to come home and avail herself of what she considered the best medical treatment. Judy hoped to appease her mother's anxiety with a show of independence. In truth, she couldn't do more than one thing at a time. She was glad to have only one set of clothes, because she wasn't always sure how to put them on properly. She was glad she didn't have to go to work or take a class, because she couldn't follow instructions. She admitted all of this to her sister, who made lists for her.

1. toothpaste on toothbrush
2. brush teeth
3. wash face
4. panties
5. bra
6. khaki jeans
7. T-shirt

She didn't need "8. comb hair," because Judy had a mass of curls that no comb could untangle. And her sister wasn't being condescending; Judy needed every detail. Risa made lists for everything, from how to take a shower to how and when to make the bed.

Judy remained at the cottage for three more months, and at no time was she without supervision. We made our schedule at home, in the United States, so that as one or two left, another would arrive. Because space was so limited, the cot came down every morning and went back up every night. If there was more than one visitor, someone would stay in the house. What we didn't know was that as each new person arrived, our own fresh grief upon seeing Judy pulled her back into the enormity of her losses.

She probably had the most difficult time when her mother-in-law, Catherine, arrived with Sharon, Mike's sister. There was so much mutual love between Catherine and Judy, and they wanted to be attentive to each other's loss, but they both had lost so much.

She probably had the easiest time with her friend Bonnie. Bonnie was her friend of the longest duration and had known Judy as a single woman, before she met Mike, before she had two children. She could help Judy reach back in time and actually have an adventure or two.

Judy preferred frantic activities to peace and solitude. She couldn't concentrate on a book or a sewing project, and she didn't want even a minute to think. She was living on funds donated from around the world and from the family. The United States Consulate had immediately informed Mike and Judy's parents when Judy was found, and offered help in any way. It was the consulate to whom Judy turned when she eventually needed a passport, but her experience in trying to replace her credit card was devastating. The questions shook her to her core. Where was your card lost? Was anything else lost with it?

Judy needed a car, as she came into Whangarei often, for her hydrotherapy, physical therapy, and psychiatric appointments at the hospital. One of the supervisors at the hospital figured out how to get her an international driver's license, when she had absolutely no identification. Two cruising friends went with Judy to an auction to assist her in the purchase of an old third-hand car. She couldn't stop her hands from shaking so badly that it was almost impossible to write the check. She had been living completely in the present, going from hour to hour, checking the next movement on her list. Buying a car implied a decision about a future, and she wasn't ready to make any decisions pertaining to future pursuits. Isabelle taught her how to drive on the "wrong side" of the road, and the fun they had in the process alleviated her misgivings.

When I arrived in New Zealand for my turn as adult supervisor, Judy greeted me with a huge hug and that fabulous smile of hers, but I could see the crushing pain in her eyes. She was very thin, and her face was drawn. Right above two new, fine vertical lines in her forehead, her hair had turned white. Just a small patch, but for me it was a badge of her bravery. I noticed she kept her bedroom door open, with a pillow propped against it. When I asked her why, she replied, "I can't let the door get the better of me, keeping me enclosed in the room in the bed."

We often went out on the deck of Babe and Ian's house to enjoy the staggeringly beautiful panoramic views. Looking in a northeast direction, we could easily see the Poor Knights cluster of islands, the remains of a once massive volcano. Farther to the south, from the back of their house, we could see the Hen and Chicken Islands. It all seemed peaceful, and Judy didn't mind the ocean views, except when a ship would steam through and take a shortcut between any of the islets and the coast, rather than take the ocean route farther offshore. Then she would get agitated, and we would go to safer territory, far from the sight of water. We went on walks around the property. The pohutukawa trees were no longer in blossom when I arrived, but the tuis, birds native to New Zealand, loved the nectar of the yellow and golden flowers on the kowhai trees. Closer to and surrounding the cottage were the ubiquitous flax, the manuka scrub, and the cabbage trees that looked like funny palms.

We went on a lot of tiki tours, the New Zealand equivalent of little adventures and side trips. We had an ongoing contest like a game of Ping-Pong; we'd throw each other sentences that contained a word or phrase unfamiliar to us but part of Judy's adopted country's vernacular. Since there were no words that would ever adequately describe what had happened to her family, why not try a new vocabulary that completely disconnected us from any of the events? "Chuffed" and "knackered" and "ranch sliders" entered our newfound dialogue. Drinking was incompatible with all the medications Judy was taking, but that didn't stop us from introducing our new favorite phrase into every conversation: "Yikes, I had one glass of wine too many, and biffed a chunky last night."

We dressed up, put on name tags (Fifi and Trixie), and went to Ian's place of business to serve cookies to a seniors' group taking a tour of his Natural Wood Creations factory and shop.

We went with Babe far up north to visit a woman who wanted to give Judy a weaving loom. We went with Ian to a fishing tournament banquet, with Judy dressed in a swordfish costume the entire time, only her red shoes visible. We went on a fund-raising 5K run with more than a hundred staff members from Whangarei Hospital. In repose, when Judy thought no one was watching, her face would collapse and she would look ravaged and absolutely haunted.

On one of our early-morning three-mile walks, we reached Wellington Bay and lay down in the grass at Matapouri Beach. It was a beautiful day with a clear blue sky and puffy clouds above. I held her hand.

"Do you ever see shapes in the clouds?" she asked.

"Not really, at least, not often, but John has taught me how to tell what kind of weather's coming by their contours," I said.

"No, I mean something else. On one of the first walks I took here, I saw in the formation of the clouds a caravan of carts, like on a merry-go-round, but in a straight line. Mike was in the first one, and he looked happy," Judy said. "Mike said to me, 'Don't worry, Judith, we're all together.'"

She went on, "He was pulling the second cart, and there was Ben, grinning, and he told me he was having fun, and told me to have fun, too. Ben was pulling the third cart, with Annie in it, and Annie was pulling a fourth cart, which was empty. Annie said to me, 'This will be for you, Mommy. But take your time, Mommy; we'll wait for you forever.'"

Judy and I were both sobbing by then, and I cradled her in my arms.

"I wouldn't even get out of bed each morning if it weren't for Mike," Judy said. "He comes to me and tells me to get up, be strong, and be happy."

Whenever we were home for dinner at the cottage, we ate on our laps in the lounge. One night I suggested that it might be more comfortable for Judy's back if she were sitting at a table.

"We could go to the next auction and get a small collapsible one," I suggested.

"No, I can't stand the thought of sitting down properly for a meal, in my own place, and no one fighting to sit beside me."

In the early months of Judy's survival, it was almost impossible for her to take comfort in kind words and deeds. She had great medical care, social services, physiotherapy, medications, and sessions with a psychiatrist, but a cure has yet to be discovered for heartbreak of this magnitude. Some days she was actually happy, delighted by her new surroundings and social activities. Some days she felt she had been condemned to go on living. Some days she just willed herself to live.

*Fifteen*

# Realities

❈

IT WAS APRIL 1996, THE DAY AFTER JUDY'S BIRTHDAY, the first one without her family, the first one with no cause for celebration. But she had been crying less and sleeping more. She felt she could finally manage the long trip to California. Perhaps it was time to seek comfort in the United States.

At Los Angeles International Airport everything seemed so familiar, but where was Mike? He should be picking her up. That was the problem with returning. Everything was too familiar. Everything reminded her of her family. Judy bent over in agony. Strangers had familiar accents and wore clothes like the ones her family would choose. She kept thinking she saw Mike or Ben or Annie among the crowds. Judy realized she was completely unprepared to resume life in her home country.

The Sleavins still had a house in the Santa Clarita Valley, about thirty-five miles northwest of Los Angeles. It was rented out but full of their belongings. Just before they left, Mike and Judy had built a shed in the backyard for storage. They put

Sheetrock on the inside and assigned a wall for each person. Ben and Annie stood against their walls while Mike drew an outline of each of them. Judy helped them fill in the outlines, painting the outfits they were wearing, discussing with excitement how big they might be when they returned. Then there were the messages they had scribbled, to be read when they completed their voyage. The burden of that memory made it impossible for Judy to return to her home.

On September 11, 2004, at an anniversary memorial service in New York City, Mayor Michael Bloomberg talked to the families still grieving for the ones they had lost in the World Trade Center. A portion of his talk went something like this: "We call a child who loses a parent an orphan, a man who loses a wife a widower, a woman who loses her husband a widow. But for a parent who loses a child, there is no name, because there are no words to describe that kind of pain."

*Sixteen*

# The Burden of Memory

❋

NO ONE WOULD HAVE BEEN SURPRISED IF SOMEONE IN
Judy's circumstances had succumbed to behavior that was out
of the ordinary or even extreme. In fact, there were a few by-
standers ready to set the stage for a dysfunctional performance.
She vividly remembers the ones who would plague her with
unfortunate questions such as "How do you get up in the morning?" "How can you keep on going?" and especially "Why didn't
you go back for Ben?"

Mostly, though, people were concerned and deferential when
she returned, but she felt unable to respond to their offers of
support and reassurance. There was no solace for her anywhere
in the United States. At the homes of relatives, she looked away
from the framed family photographs on the walls. As she drove
past the streets of strangers, she imagined cozy domestic lives,
with the evidence of tricycles and balls and pets in the yards.
It was impossible to go into a neighborhood store without re-

membering Annie's excitement over stuffed animals or Ben's leisurely examination of all the Lego sets.

Judy felt she had taken a giant step backward. In New Zealand, her psychiatrist and therapists had regularly questioned her about any suicidal feelings she might have. She had answered that her worst times were in the mornings, when she awakened with such strong memories of the children. Each morning she had to make a concerted effort to get out of bed, but she had not experienced the desire to kill herself. She wondered, though, if it was the result of the antidepressant medication or all the attention she received. She was aware that it had been enormously helpful to be in a new country where she had to forge new pathways, a country unrelated to her own history or reminiscences.

Now, in the United States, Judy realized her mental wellbeing was precarious. She didn't want to be assaulted by the memories of her old way of life at every turn. Visits with old and dear friends weren't reassuring; the conversations with them reinforced just how different she had become. Although both her mother and Mike's mother invited Judy to stay with them, she knew that would only remind her of what she had lost. She didn't want to live in her old house or her old neighborhood. She didn't even want to live in homes where her family had visited on holidays, or want to sleep in the beds they had slept in on those visits. For the first several months at home, she shut out Mike's family, especially her beloved nieces and nephews. Seeing them would trigger memories of the shrieks of laughter as they played with her own children. Her sense of what could bring peace had radically changed since the collision.

Aside from New Zealand, the only place Judy thought she

might find any peace was with Tim Rooney, Mike's best friend. Tim was more than a friend really; he had been an unofficial sibling in the Sleavin home in Tacoma when Mike was growing up. The two boys went to the same school, and Mike's dad had taught both boys how to sail. When it was time for college, Mike and Tim decided to attend the same one, Western Washington University in Bellingham, so they could be roommates. Judy had known Tim almost as long as she knew Mike. And she couldn't forget Mike's final advice in the dinghy, while she, Annie, and Mike were still together, hanging on: "If anything happens to me, call Tim. Don't worry, Judith, he'll look after you and Annie."

What Judy had wanted then, and what she wanted now, was to be with her husband. She wanted him to hold her, and to cry and grieve with her. Who but Mike would be able to comprehend and share in the depth of this terrible mourning? Only Mike would have the same hole in his heart, the same numbness in his brain, the same barren future without the children as she.

Judy thought Tim might be the only living person who could right her capsized life. Over the years, just as he had informally adopted Mike as his brother, he adopted Judy and the children as his family. He would be able to appreciate at least some of the immensity of her loss. He was brainy and handsome and sweet-natured, but he was often tormented with episodes of depression. Everyone worried that Judy might have to look after Tim.

In anticipation of Judy's arrival, Tim called me with the request that I use my professional contacts to set up an appointment with a highly recommended psychiatrist in Seattle, a forty-minute drive from Tim's home in Tacoma. He told me he was more than willing to provide refuge and companionship.

"I owe her, Hester. I loved Michael, and I can only hope that when I die I'm as happy and content doing what I have chosen. Judith helped him fulfill his cruising dream, and maybe I can help her heal," he said. "Actually, I could use some healing myself. I wrecked a wall in my home when I got the news."

Judy moved into Tim's house on Sunset Drive in Tacoma, with its beautiful view of South Puget Sound and the snow-topped Olympic Mountains. They took long walks every day. They both cried as he told her stories about Mike's childhood. In the evenings Tim played the piano or they watched videos or she told him stories about the *Melinda Lee*—not stories of the collision but of the bedtime rituals, of Ben's many questions, of Annie's wanting a puppy. Tim's yard was large and untended, overgrown with blackberry bushes and weeds, and Judy liked it that way. It made his home seem inhospitable and forbidding. She had found her hideout. Judy felt comforted and safe, and we all felt relieved. At first, they settled into an unstructured routine. Judy woke up late in the morning, they ate at unusual hours, and they left the house only to take walks, buy groceries, or rent videos. Tim had no clocks in his otherwise well-furnished home.

Tim took her to her first appointment with the psychiatrist in Seattle. That evening, in the midst of their familiar routine of eating dinner and watching a video, Judy began to sob. This time she could not stop. Perhaps she had delved into new territory in her therapy. Perhaps it was the movie itself. There was a scene in which a young girl is surprised with a birthday party. Judy can't recall if it was the sight of the cake and candles or the appearance of the little girl, but she remembers wailing in anguish and then screaming, the same inhuman, unstoppable screams she had screamed in the dinghy. Tim rocked her until the screaming stopped, and he held her while she sobbed, "They killed my babies, they killed my husband, and now they have really killed me."

All those feelings she had attempted to fend off—that her life held no meaning, that it was pointless to heal, that she had survived for nothing—came rushing in. She had nothing to celebrate, nothing to mourn. She told me later that if it had not been for Tim's patience, she probably would have killed herself. Her psychiatrist wanted to hospitalize her, but Judy was adamant about staying with Tim. She couldn't sleep, so she paced. She couldn't eat. Tim doled out all her medications, one by one. He locked up every pill in the house, and he stayed close by. When she did lie down, he brought a mattress upstairs to her room and slept on the floor next to her bed. The psychiatrist insisted on seeing Judy seven days a week, and Tim was there in the waiting room at every appointment.

She managed to muddle through her days and gradually she acquired new coping skills. Judy and Tim, with their usual humor, assigned categories for the level of care he was providing according to her mental state: babysitting was at the bottom rung, adult supervision meant a moderate amount of attention, and twenty-four-hour surveillance was full guardianship. She loved Tim's irreverence. He was the perfect protector and her willing partner in deflecting the serious issues with mockery and laughter. Judy and Tim both had a kind of impudence that got them through the daily chore of living.

Eventually, Judy was able to decrease her appointments with

the psychiatrist to several times a week, but there was a profound shift in her sense of well-being. In New Zealand, she had been frightened to take her first shower, frightened to climb the five stairs to the pool for her first hydrotherapy, frightened to leave the hospital. With each step, though, her anxiety had decreased, so she wasn't aware she was suffering from post-traumatic stress disorder until it became evident on a motor home excursion through parts of the South Island, a month before she returned to the United States.

She had been invited to accompany her friends Martha and Dana Robes, from the sailboat *Sarah Jane*. One morning Martha found Judy huddled and weeping on the floor in one of the campground showers. Judy confessed that although she could not understand why, she felt agitated each time she took a shower in the cold water. Martha and Dana took her to a hotel, and as soon as she warmed up, she made light of the episode.

When it was time for Judy to return to the United States, it was Martha and Dana who accompanied her on the long flight to Los Angeles. They had not forgotten the incident at the campground.

Following her emotional crisis over the movie with the little girl and the birthday cake at Tim's house, though, Judy's past and present experiences became inseparable. She became watchful, believing that even on dry land, a rogue wave could topple her over at any moment.

Post-traumatic stress disorder (PTSD) has become a familiar term. It was first recognized as a complex medical condition after the experiences of American soldiers in Vietnam, but any terrifying or harmful ordeal can cause this disorder. Most of us have experienced a rush of adrenaline in ordinary situations that creates nervous tension or stressful anticipation. Your heart pounds, your stomach muscles contract, you breathe more rapidly. But imagine you are confronted with a catastrophic or life-threatening situation. Your body is flooded with these stress hormones, shifting you to "fight, flight, or freeze" reactions. Blood is directed away from organs not essential to your survival and toward the large muscle groups that empower you to fight or flee. Your body is priming to defend itself. It is this cascade of adrenaline and noradrenaline that prepares you to fend off the threat. Highly regarded researchers have proposed that the longer the duration of this cascade, the more likely the events that triggered it will be imprinted on your brain. Psychiatrists call this memory consolidation. People with PTSD repeatedly relive the trauma, which in turn causes sleep problems, panic attacks, anxiety, and difficulty in concentrating.

Judy's flashbacks were horrific. Powerful and debilitating images came unbidden. She could be in a store, and suddenly her attention would be diverted by a curly head of hair like Annie's or the color red. She would drop her purchases, paralyzed. Or she could be in bed drifting off to sleep, with the window slightly open, and suddenly she was there, cold and alone in the frigid waters of the ocean rather than in the safety of her bedroom. The images were vivid and crystal clear, as if she were actually experiencing the situation in its immediacy rather than recalling it in a more muted memory. She had always been resilient, but these flashbacks brought her to her knees. She made sure to close all the windows and turn up the thermostat. She tried to eliminate any other stimuli that might slide her back into the past, but she was staggered by her mind's ability to flip that automatic switch and replicate events from the disaster, even when she was in a friendly, relaxed environment.

In her other life, her pre-collision life, Judy never had any doubts about her own determination and capabilities. She had always been resourceful, and an imaginative problem-solver. But she was strikingly ineffective in stemming these flashbacks. She had all kinds of strategies to fend them off, but she never knew when a sight, a sound, or a smell would trigger the horror. She thought of her flashbacks as gremlins scheming to occupy her mind and her body. The gremlins were also there when she walked past the kitchen knives, and they made her look at those knives; they told her how to use them to find peace and be with her husband and children. She knew she had to outwait them without doing anything dangerous. She talked aloud, wrote in a journal, went for walks or to the gym, and spent time with friends. Above all, she kept herself as warm as possible in all her activities. Cold took her back to every excruciating minute in the dinghy. Cold iced her up and shattered her heart, again and again. Some days those gremlins were altogether too seductive, and she surrendered to her grief and desolation. Some nights she wanted to die, just so she could sleep.

There was another great change. Judy once had pretty impressive organizational skills and a mind that took in ten things at once. But because of the PTSD she was unable to follow simple instructions. She had been able to toss Risa's explicit instructions of early-morning tasks, but she was unable to function without a daily list of activities. She couldn't concentrate enough to drive anywhere that included more than two turns on a straightaway road, and she got lost in a simple recipe. Her journal entries from that time reflect the impatience she felt for herself and for the advice she received from her psychiatrist. She preferred to simply recite the details of her day rather than organize those details in the larger context of managing her new life.

Judy enrolled in the Rehabilitation Program for Head Injury Patients at the Good Samaritan Hospital in Puyallup, Washington. She chose to rename it the Brain Academy. The staff was concerned for her welfare but reluctant to admit her, even for the outpatient program: the events surrounding the cause of her brain injury were so significant. They wanted her to be aware that one eight-week session would not be enough to create a successful outcome. Judy's psychiatrist persuaded them to take her in, and to limit the scope to exercises that would increase her concentration, help her organize her days, and give more structure to future goals. Their therapeutic methods and exercises gave Judy some focus and lessened her anxiety about her visual agnosia. They taught her how to use voices and hair patterns to recognize people so she wouldn't be hesitant about engaging in social activities. Her therapy included an assignment: talking to people outside her immediate, close-knit circle of friends. She had always taken her friendliness and her outgoing personality for granted. Now it was homework.

Judy loved the vocational therapy program; its intent was to give the patients an opportunity to consider suitable jobs. Judy visited quilt stores and the Almond Roca factory and dreamed of pursuing a career in the chocolate business. Her concentration skills improved when she actually designed a quilt. The flashbacks still had a huge dismantling effect on her psyche, but with the distraction of these new activities she was making some progress.

Things weren't going so well on another front. Judy had taken it for granted that she could look forward to justice at some point. She had witnessed the persistence and professionalism of the New Zealand Maritime Safety Authority as they gathered evidence about the movements of the sixty ships in the area. Just before she left for the United States, the investigation had come to a successful conclusion. Not only had the pertinent ship been found, a South Korean bulk carrier of logs, but there was conclusive scientific evidence regarding its involvement. In the United States, Judy was kept current with the step-by-step proceedings, and to begin with, the results were gratifying.

Then she got news she had never anticipated. The ship's duty officer had been arrested by his country's maritime police on a charge of accidental homicide, due to his failure to act more quickly to avoid the yacht, failure to return promptly to the scene, and failure to assist the survivors. The police requested that their government's prosecutor indict the duty officer, but he refused and dismissed all charges. According to applicable international laws, neither the United States nor New Zealand had any jurisdiction over the criminal actions of the crew. Judy was also informed it was unlikely the shipping company would take any disciplinary action against the captain or the crew members. If Judy wanted justice, she would have to file a civil lawsuit.

Over the next several months Judy met with an attorney from San Francisco who specialized in maritime law. Initially, he traveled to Tacoma for the meetings, and later, when Judy could manage, she and Tim flew to California. While in San Francisco, Judy was evaluated by a psychiatrist with an international reputation in the field of PTSD. His report read, in part, "Judith has experienced a combination of traumatic stressors that ranks with the most horrendous cases . . . reported in the world literature on PTSD." The report also acknowledged that people who were exposed to Judy's degree of initial trauma experienced intensified suicidal despair, and thus there was a "guarded prognosis." He recommended a therapy program specifically for PTSD.

Tim was very concerned about Judy. He remained with her in San Francisco and accompanied her to her medical and legal appointments. Her diminished ability to concentrate and resolve issues with the maritime attorney was making her feel desperate and dejected. Tim knew Judy had very little time before she would face a clump of stressors. There were many post-collision firsts waiting to topple her: Annie's birthday in October, Ben's at the beginning of November, the anniversary of the collision at the end of November, Mike's birthday in the middle of December, and then a festive holiday season for everyone but her. Tim was particularly impressed with the psychiatrist and told me that he was the most brilliant and kindest man he had ever met. He urged Judy to get into the psychiatrist's therapy program for PTSD.

This would have also pleased her attorney. He wanted her to move back to California, where she was a legal resident and where she could be more immediately available to discuss her case. He told Judy about the difficulties of proceeding against a shipping company outside the United States. Apparently, they could ask that Judy file the suit within their country and request her presence there. She wrote a letter to her friends in New Zealand.

*I've been evaluated by all sorts of doctors, neurophysiologists, relatives, friends, ex-boyfriends and even a golden retriever. They all come up with the same diagnosis: this woman needs a vacation.*

Judy didn't get her vacation, but she did become a nomad, traveling often between California and Washington. Her attorney had made the idea of her living in California seem so reasonable, and she didn't want to admit how apprehensive she was at the thought of starting over again. She had dear friends in the San Francisco area, and her family resided in California, but she still needed to be with Tim, who could be on call twenty-four hours a day in Tacoma.

Judy promised her attorney that she would make a permanent move to California after she completed her therapy and rehabilitation sessions in Washington. However reluctant she might be to relocate, she did want justice and authorized her attorney to file a civil lawsuit.

Judy returned to Tim's house and continued her psychotherapy in Seattle. At the end of September she completed her first eight-week rehabilitation course at the Good Samaritan Hospital in Puyallup. It was just before Annie's birthday, and she went to Colleen Polley's house to decorate cupcakes with her nieces and nephew. It was the first time she had seen them, but she knew this was exactly what Annie would have wished her to do. She called and told me that it had been fantastic, and she wondered, as Annie's godmommy, would I be interested in celebrating her birthday with Judy on October 2?

We met early in the morning, in downtown Seattle, and went to the Sheraton Hotel for breakfast. I brought a beautiful Mexican ceramic candlestick holder I had purchased for the occasion. I knew Annie would have loved it. It was bright blue and pink, with colorful ceramic flowers and birds attached, and places for three candles. We placed it on the table before us, lit the candles, and ordered from the children's menu—everything in miniature, including the muffins. We cried instead of eating and stayed for three hours, until the little candles burned down, while the waitstaff remained patient and respectful. Then we browsed through toy stores and went on the carousel at Seattle Center.

Judy and I discussed all the recent events.

"Did you get an evaluation from the Brain Academy after the first session?" I asked.

"Not a very good one," Judy replied. "They said I make decisions too quickly and change my mind too much. They said I should definitely enroll for the second session."

"Will you?" I asked.

"It would be a problem, because my attorney wants me to move back to California immediately."

I pointed out that in San Francisco she could get therapy for her PTSD. She was going to have to confront all those vivid memories in testimony, under duress, and I was afraid it would increase her flashbacks. I asked which would be worse: reliving the events of the collision in a lawsuit that could last several years, or not following through?

"I do feel I have an obligation to make them accountable, and I don't want anybody else to go through this kind of catastrophe," Judy said. "You know, I've been thinking, if I win we could start a foundation to support maritime safety. Would you help me?"

I agreed to help but reiterated my belief that her mental well-being should be her first concern.

To my surprise, Judy said, "I just realized while we've been talking exactly what I need to do to be the best witness. I'm not going to the second session at the Brain Academy or to the PTSD therapy. If the therapy is too effective, it might diminish my memory for all the details and impair my ability to help with the depositions and testimony."

I stared at her in wonder.

"Judith Ann, you are the most extraordinary person I know," I said. "This doesn't have to be final, though. Remember, you failed decision-making at the Brain Academy."

We both laughed, but I worried for her welfare.

Judy made plans to return to San Francisco in time for Ben's birthday, November 3. Bonnie, his godmother, lived there, and Judy looked forward to spending time with her. She knew her appointments with the attorney would go easier after some time with Bonnie.

Her attorneys were patient and empathetic, but the process was grueling. Judy spent her mornings reciting the facts of the collision and her afternoons weeping about the wreckage of her life. She yearned for the little cottage in Tutukaka, where she might be able to ward off the nightmares and indiscriminate memories. It was the spiritual home of her family, and that's where she felt closest to them. What was she doing away from them on the anniversary of the collision? She made a plane reservation and returned before November 24, Southern Hemisphere time.

The combined treatment of psychotherapy, cognitive behavioral therapy, and antidepressant medication decreased Judy's levels of anxiety and increased her sense of well-being. Over the years, she and I have talked about the ongoing research that has produced various successful treatment methods for PTSD. At a particularly distressing time in her life I returned with her to visit the prominent psychiatrist in San Francisco, hoping she might reconsider. He was impressed with her progress, but, in his compassionate manner, he explained how she could benefit from the most up-to-date, effective approaches and management of PTSD. Judy decided against it.

One of the enduring aspects of trauma is the tendency to relive the event. Strong people, like Judy, go over and over the experience in their minds, in an attempt to master it. And her early instincts to avoid any protocol that would lessen her effectiveness in seeking justice seemed appropriate. It also isn't difficult to understand why Judy, even now, long past any verdict, would refuse a treatment that might blunt the harshness or diminish every sight and sound. Whatever happened to Mike and Ben and Annie happened to her. She refuses to relinquish those memories. She cannot bear to think that her family would be abandoned yet again.

*Seventeen*

# Gathering the Evidence

❊

THE INVESTIGATION REALLY STARTED ON THE DAY OF
the collision, with the conscientious radio operators in the Bay
of Islands. There were often as many as 250 international boats
coming into the area in New Zealand's spring, to avoid the cy-
clones in the Tropics. Land-based volunteers monitored the VHF
marine frequencies to offer assistance and weather reports.

In Opua, the clearing port for international yachts, Dorothy
Bateman helped her husband, George, run the Opua Marine
Radio. On the day of the collision, Mrs. Bateman logged a particular exchange between a sailboat and a crew member of a
Russian ship, which she reported to the investigators. She informed them of hearing the sailboat *Magic Carpet* repeatedly
calling a ship in the vicinity on VHF radio. After fifteen minutes, someone on the ship finally responded. Chris Wagner, the
sailboat's owner, warned him that there were a number of boats
in the area heading toward Opua. Mrs. Bateman's log noted that

a second crew member on the ship, whose accent she could not determine, yelled, "Your fucking yachts shouldn't be out in this weather."

Jon and Maureen Cullen, who assisted in initiating the search for the *Melinda Lee* from Kerikeri Radio, confirmed that they heard several yachts calling ships and getting no response.

"But," Mr. Cullen later told an interviewer, "it was a scenario no different from any other night. We hear these small boats calling and calling and calling these ships and nobody responds on VHF."

Most sailboats, in addition to a watch keeper in the cockpit, kept a continuous listening watch, with their VHF radios tuned to the channel monitored by ships. As the smaller vessels, they usually took the initiative, calling large ships to make them aware of their presence. But as Mr. Cullen noted, rarely did the ships respond.

The Russian ship had departed from Auckland for Australia. The crew was contacted on the radio and questioned about the ship's location at the time of the collision. They denied any involvement. Australian authorities awaited their arrival in Melbourne, and so did the media. Many of the international newspaper articles named the ship and speculated about its involvement. The ship reported engine trouble off the coast of Australia and requested the assistance of a tug to enter the harbor, delaying their arrival. Finally the ship limped in, under the floodlights of television cameras.

The cursing of a crew member had reaped all this unwelcome attention, and then the "breaking news" footage ramped up the excitement, because easily visible on global television screens was a white paint smear across the bow of its black hull. The shipping agents who represented the owners offered "one thousand percent cooperation," and the Australian maritime authorities boarded the ship. They interviewed the master, examined the hull and the logbook. Their records established that the Russian ship was 115 miles from the scene at the time of the collision.

Jon and Maureen Cullen contacted the New Zealand Maritime Safety Authority (MSA) investigation team and told them that yachties had gathered on the sailboat *Ruquca* in Opua to provide information for the search-and-rescue operation. The investigators interviewed the group and looked at their reconstruction of the sailboat's position and the Hole in the Net entries. Chris Wagner from *Magic Carpet* reiterated the experience he and his wife had had with the Russian ship and added that they had encountered five ships en route to Opua. The investigators would have to check into the movements of all ships in the area to establish the identity of the vessel involved in the collision with the *Melinda Lee*. They would also need to determine a fairly accurate location of the collision.

On November 28, after Judy had been in the hospital just one full day, Mike Eno and Alex Livingston, two investigators from the New Zealand MSA, came to the hospital to interview Judy.

"Our condolences and our apologies. This is not very pleasant for you, but we'd like to find the ship," she recalls them saying, immediately after introductions.

Judy was quite prepared for their questions, despite her injuries. She had, after all, screamed out all the details over and over for forty-two hours in that dinghy, in her determination to tell her family's story. She was able to provide them with the *Melinda Lee*'s last position and heading, the distance from their next waypoint, the Waitangi Lead Light, and the approximate time of the collision. The investigators seemed knowledgeable and diligent, and Judy no longer felt alone in her quest for the truth.

Armed with Judy's information and with the log entries from the Hole in the Net, the New Zealand MSA began its own reconstruction of the zone of collision. The more accurately they could pinpoint the longitude and latitude, the easier it would be to establish which other vessels were in the vicinity at the same time.

Still, the New Zealand MSA had an arduous task ahead. They would have to talk to the authorities at every major port in New Zealand and look at the data of every ship leaving the country. Then, using the departure times, the investigators would have to calculate how long it would have taken each vessel to reach the collision point, given their customary cruising speeds and the routes they might have taken on the way to their stated destinations. They would also have to monitor all radio traffic from shipping in the area, including those vessels heading toward New Zealand, and those passing through the international waters off the North Island. They would have to request records from each ship and, in some cases, ask them to examine their hulls for any damage. They would have to conduct an aerial and marine search to uncover debris and ascertain how the winds and currents might have affected the location of that debris. They would have to factor in the weather conditions, with assistance from the Meteorological Service of New Zealand, located in Wellington.

The New Zealand MSA investigators eliminated fifty-nine ships before naming the South Korean–registered, 548-foot, 27,000-ton log carrier *Pan Grace* as their most likely suspect. Their calculations placed the *Pan Grace* within two nautical miles of the *Melinda Lee*'s calculated position. No other vessels were in the area at the time. Tony Martin, acting director of the New Zealand MSA, would not confirm the *Pan Grace*'s involvement, but did say it was the only ship whose crew did not respond to attempts by the MSA to contact them. The radio had been turned off.

Statements from the master of the *Pan Grace* and any crew members who were on duty—along with statements from Judy, as the only surviving witness of the *Melinda Lee*—would be necessary to establish the sequence of events. No one was interested in assigning blame until it was clear what had happened. What troubled everyone was that the *Pan Grace* had left the scene. In the words of one of the investigators in New Zealand, "They could have, at the least, reported the incident so that we might have come to aid."

Jurisdiction on the high seas is complex. There is an enormous body of laws and regulations governing both maritime safety and environmental protection. Any incident occurring within a country's territorial zone, which extends twelve nautical miles offshore, would give the country rights to at least some jurisdiction over vessels of a foreign registry.

This collision occurred some twenty-eight miles offshore. Despite the fact that New Zealand had no legal mandate and limited resources for a large-scale operation, the authorities worked assiduously to investigate all aspects of the event. Some attributed their efforts to the moral obligation to a woman who had washed up on their shores. Others attributed it to normal procedures in an inherently principled nation.

Earlier that same year, in March, a French yacht was struck by a cargo ship off the west coast of New Zealand. Although the sailors set off flares to alert the ship of their plight, it did not stop to assist the family of four aboard the yacht. Fortunately, no one was injured, and they managed to get into the nearest port, despite being dismasted and bearing a huge hole in their deck. Nine months later they were still managing the damage and repairs, but the Guiton family took the time to send Judy a letter.

"We are thinking of you every day and hope that you are recovering. We feel very close to you because of the similar event, and we have been going through all the investigation procedures, which you must be going through now. If you want to discuss anything with us or just have a talk, we would be very happy to help you."

In their case, the New Zealand MSA tracked the ship responsible for the hit-and-run to Myanmar, also known as Burma. There were problems contacting the Myanmar maritime safety authorities, and no one associated with Myanmar's ship registry would follow up. Neither the French family nor the New Zealand MSA had any recourse. Despite this, the New Zealand MSA was not discouraged when they took on the investigation of the *Melinda Lee* collision, and their dedication was undeniable.

In a press briefing, Tony Martin, acting director of the New Zealand MSA, noted that the *Pan Grace* could not be compelled to disclose its records. If the ship refused to respond, there would be no recourse. It might, he said, be possible to appeal to colleagues in the South Korea maritime authority for their cooperation.

Early in December, the New Zealand MSA requested limited authority to act on behalf of the United States. New Zealand law does not empower their MSA to investigate accidents that occur outside territorial waters between one or more non–New Zealand ships. Under the United Nations Convention on the Law of the Sea (UNCLOS), it is the exclusive jurisdiction of the flag state (the country where the ship is registered) to investigate a marine casualty or incident of navigation that causes loss of life or serious injury to nationals of another flag state.

This upset John Sleavin, Mike's brother. He and his mother spoke with several maritime attorneys who confirmed the complexities that occur in dealing with a foreign-flagged vessel outside territorial waters. John recalls one maritime attorney asking them, "If a ship built in Canada, owned by a New York firm, registered in Panama, with a multinational crew, caused death and destruction at sea, where do you think an investigation and trial might be held?"

"In the country of the victims?" John guessed.

"Unlikely," the attorney said.

"In the United States?" John tried again. "The owners in New York should have some responsibility for who gets hired, and if their crew is inexperienced and causes mayhem."

"Only if the New York owners registered the ship in the United States. Owners elect where to register their ships. So, in this hypothetical case, Panama would have to conduct the investigation," the attorney said.

"The country where the ship is registered is known as the flag state," he continued, "and it is entirely lawful to register a ship outside the country of ownership. So most ships fly a flag of a country other than the country of ownership. They're known as flags of convenience. The two most common are Panama and Liberia. The law of registration governs the internal affairs. Some flag states have very conscientious practices and are willing to enforce strict international standards, but the ones who ignore their responsibilities create problems: safety, environmental, and labor issues, to name a few. Economic incentives, such as low taxes and the ability to hire cheap multinational crew, are often the reason owners choose flags of convenience."

"But we're not talking flag of convenience here," John said. "The *Pan Grace* is owned and registered in South Korea, and it's my understanding that it was manned entirely by a South Korean crew."

"South Korea is one of the only countries that has more home flags than foreign ones," the attorney said. "That's a good thing. It means that the ship, its master and crew will be easy to find and interview. They won't be scattered all over the globe."

"But does that mean my sister-in-law would have to go to trial in South Korea?"

"Entirely possible," the attorney replied.

"But what if the South Korean government has its own agenda and decides it wants to protect its shipping companies?" John asked.

"Then they won't prosecute. It could even be contended that any civil suit brought by your family should be argued in South Korean courts," the attorney said.

"Right now all I'm concerned about is Judy's welfare, and gathering evidence," John said. "The New Zealand MSA said there would be no recourse if the *Pan Grace* refused to disclose their records."

"As I said, it's complex, but basically that is true. They can cooperate with New Zealand and the United States, or not. It's in their court, so to speak, and they can shut down or open up," the attorney said.

"So, in effect, my brother's murderer gets to decide whether or not to put himself on trial," John said. His frustration was palpable.

John Sleavin was grateful to the New Zealand MSA for its thoroughness in tracking down the *Pan Grace*. He knew that it was too much to assume they would send a representative to South Korea to await the arrival of the *Pan Grace*, which was expected to dock in Inchon on December 11. Additionally, he felt strongly about having a United States presence in Inchon. John lived in Portland, Oregon, and contacted the United States Coast Guard there. It was suggested that he call the U.S. Coast Guard Marine Safety Office in Hawaii, since that office might have more information about an investigation taking place in the South Pacific.

John reached Lieutenant Commander Bob Acker in Honolulu. Acker told John it was unlikely that the Coast Guard would be involved in the investigation in another country, save for a United States–flagged commercial vessel, in some exceptions. Acker told him the Coast Guard had already done as much as it could; they had evaluated and dismissed a possible suspect vessel that entered American Samoa with a damaged hull.

Beyond that, the United States Coast Guard had granted the request of the New Zealand MSA to continue the investigation on their behalf, based upon the UNCLOS resolution. However, John was informed, the New Zealand investigators definitely would not be going to South Korea; the authority granted to them was limited to reasonable actions deemed necessary in determining the cause of the *Melinda Lee* incident.

John had always been involved in advocacy issues, from bicycling paths to light rail, and he understood what a concerted effort by the Sleavin siblings could do. He talked to them about using diplomatic channels to increase the possibility of United States participation in the investigation. His sister Peg lived in Oregon, his sister Colleen lived in Washington state, his sister Kathy lived in Colorado, and his sister Sharon lived in Alexandria, Virginia. If they all contacted their respective members of Congress, surely it would result in some congressional action.

Sharon's state representative in Virginia was Jim Moran, and her state senator was John Warner. On December 8, with time running out before the *Pan Grace* would dock in its home port, she faxed both offices thirteen pages of information and articles. Sharon was told that Senator Warner had been in the navy in the Second World War, and he might offer the best support. In fact, Senator Warner had disrupted his law school education for active military duty on the Korean Peninsula in 1951, a year after the Korean War broke out. He also had completed a bachelor of science in engineering degree. He had more in common with Judy than he would ever know.

In 1995, when his office was contacted, Senator Warner was the vice chairman of the Senate Intelligence Committee. His actions on behalf of his constituent Sharon Sleavin MacDonald, in the Commonwealth of Virginia, and on behalf of her family, reflected his reputation for being conscientious and fairminded. Senator Warner ensured that the United States Coast Guard would become involved with the investigation and that one of its officers would be waiting on the dock for the *Pan Grace* to arrive. Within several days, Acker in Honolulu was directed by U.S. Coast Guard headquarters in Washington, D.C., to oversee the investigation from Honolulu and to assign an officer from their Marine Safety Office in Asia to head to South Korea immediately. His presence would be supported by the International Maritime Organization Resolution A.637(16), which establishes procedures for member countries to cooperate in marine casualty investigations, and to share information, where they have a substantial interest.

The *Pan Grace* did not come directly into port. It remained at an anchorage just outside the harbor. The shipping company, Pan Ocean, sent its own inspector and a company lawyer out to the ship. Company representatives sent back several inconsistent messages: Pan Ocean initially reported traces of fiberglass, scratches, and paint markings on the bow of the *Pan Grace*, but later the ship denied having been in the area of the collision.

"Scratches are common," said a company spokesman.

The *Pan Grace* had been given clearance to dock and unload the cargo, but the ship remained at anchor.

"The ship is mooring off the port awaiting required procedures," said its spokesman.

Eric Matthews, the United States Coast Guard officer, took a launch out to look at the hull of the *Pan Grace*. He noted several areas of paint and scratches and he photographed them as the launch circled twice, but he was not allowed to board the ship or even get too close.

The evidence seemed suspicious; the photographs showed the paint scratches on the *Pan Grace*'s hull to be the same color blue as the antifouling paint on the *Melinda Lee*. However, it was circumstantial evidence, and the *Pan Grace* could easily maintain that the scratches were made by their own anchor or anchor chain, or the ship bumping the wharf in Tauranga, New Zealand, before they departed. In fact, while some of the crew said they could not account for the scratches, several crew members said the hull was "not in good shape" when they left Tauranga, despite a recent painting. Without the *Melinda Lee* (which was at the bottom of the ocean), there was no paint available to compare to the transferred paint. Indeed, a Pan Ocean representative sent a list of questions, and the top three were: Where is the *Melinda Lee*? What is the state of the *Melinda Lee*'s condition? and Will the *Melinda Lee* be raised? The Pan Ocean Shipping Company could be looking for a way to refute all the evidence.

Both issues—proving the scratches and paint markings on the *Pan Grace* occurred after the ship departed from its last port in New Zealand, and identifying the source of those paint transfers as the *Melinda Lee*—were solved in the most improbable ways.

The newspapers had been reporting the progress, or lack thereof, with headlines such as KOREANS STALL OVER SHIP EVIDENCE. In New Zealand, a letter was delivered to the Whangarei Hospital for Judy, from Camlab Colour Limited in Tauranga.

> *Dear Mrs. Sleavin,*
>
> *My deepest sympathy for your tragic loss. Enclosed are two photographs of the Pan Grace as she left Tauranga Harbour on 23 November 1995. I cannot see any marks on the bow, and to confirm this, I have enlarged a portion of the negative. Please use the prints if they are of any benefit. The negatives belong to Howard Dunn, whose hobby is to photograph commercial ships when they enter or leave from Tauranga.*
>
> *Yours sincerely,*
> *Adria E. Cameron*

We were all grateful to Howard Dunn, the retired gentleman whose interests in shipping and photography were invaluable to Judy, and we blessed Adria Cameron, the proprietress of the camera shop, whose hobby surely could have been in the amateur detective field. The photographs proved irrefutably that when the *Pan Grace* left Tauranga, the ship's last port before the collision, she left with a clean hull, devoid of scratches and markings or paint transfers.

The second problem was more difficult to solve. A Royal New Zealand Air Force Orion went out again, over a region of 1,500 square miles, on a recovery search for the bodies and the

wreckage of the *Melinda Lee.* A shoreline search was conducted as well. Marine experts had warned that it was highly
improbable the bodies would come ashore with the weather
conditions and prevailing currents. They also explained that
"due to the depth of the water and the pressure of the cold, it
would be extremely debatable whether the bodies could float
up." Nevertheless, the trained spotters were optimistic that they
might sight pieces of the hull for the evidence the investigation
required. They did find some flares and some metal canisters,
most likely from the Sleavins' life raft, but there were no rem-
nants of the hull itself.


None of the yachties in Opua or Whangarei had been in Trinidad when the Sleavins had purchased their antifouling paint,
in bulk, with a number of cruisers. Annique asked Judy if she
could remember any of the other cruisers who had used that
same bottom paint, because if they could be found, they might
be persuaded to send in samples from their boats. Judy thought
maybe their dear friends Peter and Glenda Couch had been
part of the group that purchased the paint. She thought Peter
and Glenda might be in North Carolina on their sailboat, *Lamorna.* They had said goodbye to the Sleavins in Venezuela and
sailed to Puerto Rico, planning to make their way up the East
Coast of the United States. Judy also told Annique to be gentle
when she told them about the tragedy; they had been Ben and
Annie's surrogate grandparents for eight months.

Peter and Glenda were indeed in North Carolina, and at the
same time Judy and Annique were figuring out a way to contact them, they heard the terrible news from good friends on

another boat nearby. Their friends had access to a phone, and Glenda called Judy at the hospital. Judy was thrilled to hear her voice. They cried together and then, Judy recalls, she told a startled Glenda they would have to mourn later, right now she needed help with the investigation. Had they bought the same antifouling paint as the Sleavins in Trinidad, she asked Glenda, and if not, did they remember any of the cruisers who had? The Couches had not, but offered to get on the ham radio and put out a worldwide call asking for the information. A ham operator soon relayed a reply from Sherry and Lenny Beckett, who were still in Trinidad on their boat, *Island Time*. Sherry went to the boatyard, asking if the owners might supply her with the invoices or names of everyone who had been part of the bulk purchase of the Ameron blue antifouling paint that had been used on the *Melinda Lee* in 1994. The boatyard personnel found a copy of the Sleavin invoice and passed it on to the paint manufacturer. The manufacturing warehouse was searched to find the antifouling paint with the exact matching date code, and a wet sample was provided. The paint manufacturer ensured that the paint went directly to the United States Coast Guard. The boatyard personnel then directed Sherry and Lenny to the sailboat *Nereides* from Gothenburg, Sweden. Rolf Berg had just hauled his boat out for maintenance. He was happy to allow them to chip some paint samples from *Nereides'* bottom, from paint with the same date code, bought at exactly the same time the Sleavins had bought theirs for the *Melinda Lee*.

It was a confluence of factors that led to gathering all the evidence. Later we would learn that this was the simple part.

*Eighteen*

# The Investigation

✵

THE NEW ZEALAND MARITIME SAFETY AUTHORITY HAD
sent a communication to the port authority in Inchon, South
Korea, apprising them of the impending arrival of the *Pan
Grace* and of its probable involvement in a collision. They also
notified their maritime safety counterparts in Seoul that the
New Zealand investigators had been granted limited authority
on behalf of the United States, and they appealed for full cooperation. They asked the Korean Central Marine Accident Inquiry Agency (CMAIA) to question the master and crew of the
ship and share the responses. The New Zealand MSA would
also interview Judy over a course of several weeks, asking for
more and more detailed information.

The United States Coast Guard's role was more informal, as
their findings could not be entered as evidence in a court of
law. They were there to support the Korean investigators in
their efforts, to represent the United States, and to verify that a
thorough and complete investigation was being done.

The Honolulu office of the Coast Guard sent Chief Warrant Officer Eric Matthews to South Korea from his post in Japan. He was experienced in the area of ships and shipping, and well acquainted with the formalities in Asia. In fact, earlier that year, he had been assigned to Ulsan, South Korea, to conduct the required annual safety inspections of United States–flagged vessels hauled out in the shipyards there for maintenance. Matthews met with the personnel at the United States Embassy in Seoul, read all the reports the New Zealand investigators had sent, and then went to Inchon to meet with the chief investigator and staff of the Inchon District Marine Accident Inquiry Agency (MAIA). He asked for access to all related files. They declined, but suggested he contact the United States Embassy in Seoul; it was the beginning of many circuitous routes Matthews would have to take to obtain information. The MAIA did take him to catch a launch to look at the hull of the *Pan Grace*, anchored out a number of miles. The vessel was still loaded with logs when he circled twice and took photographs.

The United States Embassy asked the South Korean authorities to send the U.S. Coast Guard copies of documents containing the responses of the crew members to questions sent them by the New Zealand investigators. However, the authorities were not forthcoming.

"The responses to questions sent by New Zealand MSA to the crew are still being worked on," Matthews was told by memorandum.

Eventually Matthews received a document, in Korean. The Inchon investigators refused to help with the translation. They told him to go back to the embassy and hire a translator.

He did. The document revealed that the Inchon investigators

had interviewed the master of the *Pan Grace*, Captain Kim; Second Mate Han, who was the duty officer on watch; and Quartermaster Lee, who was at the helm of the ship. The second mate said he saw a red light from a vessel off the ship's starboard bow, but would not provide a rough estimate of the bearing of the vessel or its distance from the *Pan Grace*. He also refused to say what the visibility was during the period in question. Publicly, at least, the Inchon investigators were not disturbed by his lack of information, or even skeptical.

The *Pan Grace* remained at an anchorage just outside the harbor. Matthews requested a launch to look at the hull more closely, but his request was denied. The United States Embassy made a formal request to the other investigating authority, the South Korean Maritime Police. They agreed to take him out, but left him standing at the dock. Eventually someone came by to tell him the Maritime Police had decided at the last minute to go out to the *Pan Grace* an hour before the appointed time.

While the Investigations Branch of the United States Coast Guard in Washington, D.C., and Lieutenant Commander Acker in Honolulu, had the bulk of the administrative burden, Matthews was willing to monitor any activities related to the *Pan Grace*. It was very challenging to get any cooperation, but he was determined to stand by to ensure that the hull was not repainted.

Finally, the *Pan Grace* proceeded to port to unload its cargo of logs. Matthews was allowed to be in attendance, accompanied by the Maritime Police. He observed several areas of distinct blue markings on the hull and recent, sweeping scratches from the sea surface up to the center and over to the starboard side. When the cargo was offloaded and the bow rose higher, more scratches appeared. With the evidence apparent, Matthews asked the Maritime Police to request a meeting with the master, second mate, and quartermaster. The Maritime Police declined. Matthews then asked for samples of the blue paint on the hull of the *Pan Grace*. They declined. He asked to board the ship and examine the equipment. They declined, but allowed Matthews to observe their removal of paint scrapings.

Matthews contacted the United States Embassy. He asked them to intercede with written requests to both the CMAIA and the Maritime Police. It was reasonable to ask for paint samples as well as interviews. The U.S. Embassy was told the U.S. Coast Guard and the New Zealand MSA would be sent the results of the South Korean chemical analysis of the paint, but not the paint samples themselves.

More communications were sent—by the New Zealand chief investigator, by the U.S. Coast Guard, and by the U.S. Embassy—requesting interviews with the crew and samples for independent analysis. These requests also were denied. But the South Korean Maritime Police did accept the original samples of Ameron blue antifouling paint, sent from the United States Coast Guard to the South Korean Embassy in Washington, D.C.

On January 16, Lieutenant Commander Acker, Honolulu's senior investigating officer, sent a letter to the South Korean Embassy in Washington, D.C., asking for crew responses and the results of the analysis. He sent another letter on February 27, with the same requests. He asked the maritime attaché at the South Korean Embassy in Washington, D.C., to hasten the proceedings. The attaché apologized and told him he had not heard from the investigating authorities in South Korea.

The South Korean investigators refused to turn over the results of the chemical analysis of the paint samples. Later, when a South Korean Maritime Police investigator was interviewed, he said they rejected the request by the United States Coast Guard for the paint sample because, they said, "we are the ones investigating the suspects."

Instead, the South Korean chief investigator sent a long list of questions to Acker, to be forwarded to Judy. The U.S. Coast Guard was told the South Korean authorities would refuse further communication until they received all her responses. Many of the questions had already been answered in a packet sent to them by the New Zealand MSA. The additional information they asked for, such as charts and logs, was perverse. They obviously knew everything was at the bottom of the sea.

The break came on March 14, when the Korean National Institute for Scientific Investigation announced their laboratory findings. Three means of testing were conducted: microscopic examination, acid-solvent testing, and infrared spectrophotometer testing. All three confirmed that the transferred paint on the *Pan Grace*'s hull matched the antifouling paint used on the *Melinda Lee*.

A copy of the results was released to the United States Coast Guard in Honolulu on April 10, but most likely only because a South Korean reporter for the Associated Press had written an article on April 2 describing the findings. Ultimately, paint samples from the hull were independently tested in both New Zealand and Japan, with the same conclusive results. The *Pan Grace* was undeniably the vessel involved in the collision with the *Melinda Lee*.

Despite the irrefutable scientific evidence, as soon as the results of the chemical analysis were released, the Pan Ocean company spokesman issued a statement saying they were confident the *Pan Grace* was not involved.

Pan Ocean is the second-largest shipping line in South Korea, and has offices and shipping agents in the United States. The United States and South Korea do billions of dollars in trade each year; economics, diplomatic pressure, the presence and persistence of a United States Coast Guard officer, and the international media spotlight on a family tragedy undoubtedly helped pressure the South Korean officials into conducting an investigation.

Questioning the crew, the South Korean investigating authorities determined that the second mate had seen a red light off the starboard bow of the *Pan Grace* at approximately "a one o'clock position." He recognized that the red light meant he was observing the port side of a crossing vessel, and that the *Pan Grace* was the "give-way" vessel, under the IMO's International Regulations for Preventing Collisions at Sea (known as COLREGS). Under Rule 15 of these regulations, he was to take action to avoid the *Melinda Lee,* the "stand-on" or privileged vessel. He said that at first he needed binoculars to see the red light, but soon he could see it with the naked eye. He said that upon seeing it he did not alter course to keep clear. Or tell the engine room to slow down or stand by. Or call for a lookout to go out on the bridge wing. Or go out himself for a closer look. Or locate the vessel on radar. Or call the other vessel on the VHF radio. Or sound the ship's horn. Or call the master for advice. He finally decided to take the bearing of the red light, but was unable to do so. He did realize that the *Melinda Lee* remained at the same relative bearing to the *Pan Grace,* and he understood that this indicated they were on a collision course. He did not turn on the automatic radar plotting aid, which, in conjunction with the radar, could have automatically calculated an alteration in course to avoid collision. In fact, he made no calculations before he finally decided it was time to avoid the other vessel. He simply ordered the helmsman to turn 10 degrees to starboard.

Later, under deposition, the second mate would say that because he could not detect the *Melinda Lee* on radar, he "could not think of the distance" of the *Melinda Lee* from the *Pan Grace.* He would add that he determined the 10-degree rudder change to starboard was sufficient to avoid a collision based "purely up to the watchkeeping officer's own judgment." His order to the helmsman resulted in the *Pan Grace*'s turning right into the *Melinda Lee.*

Official findings by the South Korean authorities held the *Pan Grace* accountable for the collision. According to the Korean CMAIA, the *Melinda Lee* was sighted by the *Pan Grace* far enough away, giving the second officer sufficient time to avoid the *Melinda Lee.* Among other issues, the report cited the *Pan Grace*'s apparent failure to properly detect the contact on radar, and failure to immediately decrease speed and execute a turn after visually detecting the red light ahead.

The United States Coast Guard did a comprehensive study and drew on all of the investigative reports to cite the *Pan Grace* as the "proximate cause of collision." Their report cited the *Pan Grace*'s failure, as the give-way vessel, to follow COLREGS. Adherence to a number of the rules, the report said, would have prevented the incident:

- They should have posted a lookout forward of the bridge to make a full appraisal of the situation.
- They should have posted a lookout with training in the proper use of radars.
- They should have established communication, by radio and sound signals, when they sighted the red light, in order to relay their intentions.
- They should have contacted the engine room to reduce speed and to prepare to come to "all stop."
- They should have checked that all navigation equipment, such as lights, were in proper operation at each watch.

The United States Coast Guard's report also cited a "contributing cause":

Failure to maintain a proper lookout on both the give-way and stand-on vessels.

Rule 5 of COLREGS emphasizes the need for vessels to keep a lookout at all times and states, in part, that the lookout should be kept "by sight, and hearing, and by all available means."

Mike and Judy had strict rules: one of them was always in the cockpit keeping watch, day and night. Farther out at sea, course-plotting was done every three hours, at the watch change. Closer to land, the watch keeper charted their course on an hourly basis. International regulations state that "the watch keeper shall have no other duties."

This regulation was of relevance in a fairly recent event, when a cruise ship and a container ship collided in the English Channel. After an investigation, the primary blame was placed on the officer standing watch on the cruise ship's bridge. He was overburdened and distracted by duties other than watch-keeping, including routine clerical tasks. At the time of the collision he was signing off on the garbage log.

On yachts the size of the *Melinda Lee,* the crew most often is comprised of two adults, which makes it necessary for the person on watch to also perform the navigation duties. Judy went below; that is a fact. After seeing and hearing nothing, at about 0205 she went below to obtain and chart the *Melinda Lee*'s position. Sometime between 0205 and 0212, when Judy was preparing to return to the cockpit, the *Pan Grace* rammed the *Melinda Lee.*

Had Judy seen any navigation lights, she would not have gone below for her hourly charting. Had there been any navigation lights on the *Pan Grace,* Judy would have seen the ship at least five miles away, the required distance for the lights of a ship that size to be visible. Taking into account the speed and bearing of both vessels, and using the law of cosines, Judy should have been able to see the *Pan Grace* for 25.47 minutes before the collision—at least fifteen minutes before she went below. Under deposition later, the second mate was asked if he checked that the navigation lights were on before coming on duty, and he replied, "I think I didn't."

Had Judy heard any sounds, she would not have gone below. On the *Melinda Lee,* the Sleavins kept two VHF radios on, one in the cockpit and one in the cabin at the navigation table, both tuned to channel 16, the all-purpose emergency channel. Both had a range up to twenty-five miles. No one hailed the sailboat by radio. The *Melinda Lee* also had a radar detector. Had the radar aboard the *Pan Grace* been in operation, its microwave transmission would have activated the *Melinda Lee*'s collision avoidance radar detector (CARD), causing the resounding of a loud alarm, from a distance of twelve miles.

The Sleavins knew their CARD was operable. They had heard its alarm many times. Apparently the radar on the *Pan Grace* was not on. Make no mistake: it was a modern ship with all the required equipment, and South Korea is a progressive country with established maritime academies. They did admit that the automatic radar plotting aid was not in operation. The two crew members on duty either didn't know how to use radar or did not even bother to monitor it. In testimony later, the quartermaster, who was at the helm of the ship, was unable to name or describe the function of many of the basic instruments on the bridge.

Now, more than ten years later, it might be difficult for sailors to remember the cumbersome, stationary, power-hungry cathode-ray tube radar units that were the only option for sailboats. In 1995, in addition to the usual bank of gel cell batteries, the *Melinda Lee* had solar panels, a wind generator, an engine, and a portable generator; and still, they had to be judicious in their use of radar.

The evolution of laptop computers has enhanced the liquid crystal display technology of the radar units. These days, sailors can leave radar units on in standby mode, without worrying about power consumption. The units are resistant to moisture, and they have glare-free screens. They have gimballed mounts to keep them level, whatever the sea conditions. There is electronic charting available. These days, it is not necessary to leave the cockpit for navigation purposes.

The Sleavins knew that their radar reflector, mounted high on the mast, was effective in increasing the *Melinda Lee*'s visibility on a ship's radar. It was proven as they sailed through the navy embargo off the Haitian coast, and later, most ships they spoke to on VHF radio reported seeing their boat on radar at least five miles away, even in poor conditions. Still, they knew it was more important to sight a ship before it sighted them.

The *Melinda Lee*'s established course of action in the case of another ship being in the area went something like this: they would sight the ship or its navigation lights, or in many cases first know that a ship was some twelve miles away when the alarm of their CARD sounded. This would alert them to go to a double-handed watch system—one below at the radar unit, one in the cockpit. They would call the ship on channel 16 and give their position relative to the ship's position. Even in crossing situations where the *Melinda Lee* was the "stand-on, privileged" vessel, they would offer to make a course alteration to avoid any risks, once they had made their intentions clear in a radio discussion. The *Pan Grace* did not give them any opportunity to take evasive action.

Sophisticated technology has been introduced for all kinds of systems on both commercial vessels and recreational craft. On many commercial vessels this has meant a steady reduction in the number of officers and crew manning a ship, with an over-reliance on technology. What's more, a critical tangent to the increase in shipping worldwide and the expansion of the cruise industry is the number of crew necessary to run all these ships. Often cheap labor from developing countries is hired, with no substantial training and little or no proficiency. Technology without understanding is useless.

The popularity of offshore cruising and passage-making increased with the advent of GPS. Since then, many more technological systems have been made available for recreational vessels. Although some modern devices are hard to resist, not all are essential, and some actually get in the way of developing safe practices and good seamanship skills. Some get in the way of enjoying and becoming part of the natural elements and the experiences of sailing. In difficult situations, common sense and experience can count for a lot more than complex automated systems. I imagine even Captain Cook would not have been foolish enough to turn down GPS as he explored the world, but not without his trusty sextant. Offshore sailors need to have some knowledge of navigation techniques without power requirements in the case of a breakdown or an electronic malfunction. Sailors also need to understand that equipment such as a collision avoidance radar detector and radar guard alarms are dependent upon the functionality of other vessels' equipment. Certainly there have been many reports and anecdotes about radar units on ships deliberately turned off, and not just on substandard vessels, although the reasons are unclear.

The Korean CMAIA report said the second mate had sufficient time to avoid the *Melinda Lee* when he first spotted their red light, but failed to take action until it was too late. The *Pan Grace* not only contributed to the "direct cause of the accident, but also shut down any chance to rescue the victims."

*Shut down any chance to rescue the victims.* That, perhaps, is the official term for nautical hit-and-run. Ben's death might have been attributed to inexperience or negligence. But whatever had gone wrong was egregiously compounded with the next measures taken and not taken. South Korea is a signatory to the United Nations Convention on the Law of the Sea; it is an agreement that provides for rescue and assistance to save a life, as long as the ship itself is not put in harm's way. Certainly there was no risk to the *Pan Grace*. There was speculation that Judy was mistaken in her assertions that the ship returned. It was proposed that the ship was in some kind of a skid in its attempt to get back on course. Possibly. But why had they altered course? There were conjectures that even if they were looking out the windows, it was impossible for them to actually see the two adults and one tiny girl. It would have been impossible to see the family because the crew didn't use any searchlights or any other means to look for them.

I have no doubt that the Sleavins saw the crew in the dim accommodation lights. I talked to Judy before any vessel was implicated. When I told her about the Russian ship that everyone was waiting for in Australia, Judy disagreed.

"Russian? No, I don't think so. All the men had short, dark hair, and they looked Asian," she said.

I was aghast. "They were close enough that you could see them that well?"

The readouts of the course recorder on the *Pan Grace* could have ended the dispute about the ship's movement after the collision. The course recorder on a ship is the marine equivalent of the airplane's black box. The ship's course is transmitted from the vessel's gyrocompass to the course recorder, thus providing accurate information about the course and any changes in rudder angle. The crew reported that there had been a seventeen-hour paper jam in the ship's course recorder, coincidentally beginning approximately three hours before the collision.

The New Zealand MSA sent a letter to the South Korean CMAIA:

> *We would appreciate hearing from you on what steps you have been able to take in order to check as to the cause of the course recorder's failure. Should you need any assistance on this matter, we can recommend an expert in the United Kingdom who has conducted numerous interpolations of course recorder traces following a collision. For instance, he has been able to determine, by reference of the original trace, whether the failure of the course recorder was accidental or a deliberate act. Please let us know if you wish to receive further information about this expert.*

The South Korean investigators never requested the help of the course recorder expert, but later, under oath during the depositions, some of the crew admitted to knowing of an alteration of the course recorder pens, producing a discrepancy of 10 to 12 degrees between the course recorder reading before the collision and the deck log entries of the heading of the *Pan Grace* according to the gyrocompass. It was implied in the crews' depositions that Captain Kim himself had manipulated the readings.

Captain Kim, even under oath, claimed to know nothing about events of November 24 until he was contacted by fax on December 5 by the Pan Ocean Shipping Company. However, the day after the collision, he scheduled emergency steering drills. Two days later, he made a log entry with night orders to all crew to look out for vessels bound for New Zealand and "do give-way action in advance." There was a subsequent night order prohibiting Second Mate Han from being on watch alone in inclement weather. Captain Kim had failed to make any entry in the master's night order log until after the collision.

The chief investigator in South Korea told a newspaper reporter that he had long been convinced the *Pan Grace* was involved. He waited to forward the case for prosecution, he said, until the Korean National Institute for Scientific Investigation completed chemical tests on the antifouling paint that confirmed the positive match.

South Korean Maritime Police formally booked Second Mate Han, as duty officer, on charges of accidental homicide and requested that the South Korean prosecutor's office indict him. The completed files were forwarded to the prosecutor's office on April 1, 1996.

Pan Ocean was intractably opposed to any outside directives, and a spokesman for the shipping company issued a statement that said the South Korean Maritime Police had no authority over them. Several days later, all criminal charges were dismissed by the prosecutor's office.

The Korean Maritime Board held a hearing, and the second mate had his license suspended for three months. The master was given an admonition. Pan Ocean Shipping Company changed the name *Pan Grace* to *Pan Leader* and sent the ship back out to sea for its next load of cargo.

## Nineteen

## Aotearoa

☸

JUDY SAVED HERSELF THROUGH SHEER GUTS AND IN-conceivable mental resolve, and then New Zealand saved her again, in so many ways. There was the excellent care she received at a modern hospital with a compassionate director and a professional staff. The diligence and perseverance of the New Zealand Maritime Safety Authority. The kindness and generosity of new friends. The empathy and support of strangers. The astonishing physical beauty of the country. The general goodwill. The twist on the English language, with vowels stretched well beyond their capacity. The idioms. The spirituality. The infusion of Maori culture. The land of the long white cloud.

The slower-paced, holistic sense of life gave Judy some context for her grief. Even early on in the hospital, she came to realize that here she would not have to isolate herself or suppress her anguish. The first time a nurse came to wheel her outside for some fresh air, Judy was anxious.

"I don't think I'm ready to go outside," she said. "What if I start crying?"

"I'll cry with you," the nurse replied.

"The whole of New Zealand is like a small town in mourning," wrote a local newspaper columnist. Through a representative, Judy sent out her heartfelt thanks, and after her message was read on television, there was a new outpouring of sentiment. One letter said:

> *Paul Holmes read your message to all New Zealand on TV, and I just can't stop thinking of you. Know that the country's thoughts and prayers are with you; you show a tremendous courage and sound so, so brave.*

The *New Zealand Herald*, the country's largest newspaper, reported on Thursday, November 30, 1995:

> *Yesterday, a kaumatua [elder], Mr. Walter Mountain from Rawhiti, near the spot where Mrs. Sleavin was washed ashore at Deep Water Cove, announced a rahui as a mark of respect for those lost. The rahui places a tapu [taboo] on the taking of all fish and shellfish from an area on the seaward side of the line between Tikitiki (Ninepin Island) and Rakaumangamanga (Cape Brett) for the next fourteen days. Meanwhile, marine investigators continued the inquiry.*

The Polynesians were unparalleled seafarers. Hundreds of years before European oceanic exploration began, they sailed across vast uncharted seas in their voyaging canoes. They guided these canoes, made of tree trunks and coconut fibers, over great distances using the stars, the sun, the shape of the clouds, the wind, and the direction of the currents and swells to steer their course. Their discovery and settlement is represented by the Polynesian Triangle, with Hawaii at its Northern Hemisphere apex, and Easter Island and New Zealand forming the east and southwest corners of the base in the Southern Hemisphere. Islands within this triangle are hundreds, and often thousands, of miles apart. The Polynesian Maori settled Aotearoa (New Zealand) around the year 1000, or possibly earlier.

Europeans first saw Aotearoa in the seventeenth century. In 1642, Abel Tasman, the Dutch East India Company explorer, sighted the gorgeous coastline of the South Island but was discouraged from landing by the Maori. Afterward, the Dutch named the area after one of their own provinces, Zeeland. A century later the British and French took some interest, and Captain Cook, the great English navigator, arrived in 1769. By that time, Whangarei, Judy's first home, was a thriving Maori settlement. The first European settler, William Carruth, arrived in that district in 1839.

The early city was a trading post, but what really increased the population and prosperity of the Whangarei District was the kauri timber and its gum. The magnificent trees, unique to New Zealand, were used internationally in the shipbuilding industry and for residential homes, and the gum was prized as a varnish. Maori had used the soot from burning the gum as a pigment for the dark colors of their illustrious tattoos; it also made a good fuel for cooking and, when lit, a good torch. There are still several Gumdiggers Cafés in the Northland, named as a tribute to those who worked so hard with spears and spades to excavate the gum until there was no more. Then came coal mining, wheat and dairy farming, shipbuilding, and brick making. For years, the town's progress was impeded by limited access, but the North Island Main Trunk Line from Auckland to the Bay of Islands was completed in 1923. With the first all-weather road to Auckland developed in 1934, new industries could establish themselves. The hospital to which Judy was taken stands on its original 1898 site.

New Zealand comprises two large main islands, North and South Islands, and several outlying islands. It is similar in size to the state of Colorado and lies at latitudes south of the equator similar to California's position north of the equator. January and February are the warmest months; July is the coldest. Unlike its closest neighbor, Australia, which is nearly bisected by the Tropic of Capricorn, New Zealand has warm subtropical areas in the north and cool temperate climates in the far south. It is home to beaches and lush pastoral land, fjords, rainforests, and glaciers.

When Judy arrived, at the end of 1995, New Zealanders were fond of citing the fact that the total population consisted of 3 million people and 70 million sheep. The more accurate count was 3.5 million people. Compare that with Japan, a country not much larger, with a population of 125.5 million at the time. Perhaps the slight population gives New Zealanders the good sense to make connections with others. They deserve their international reputation for hospitality and friendliness. Most stores close every day at five or six P.M., and from noon on Saturday until Monday morning. While New Zealanders are industrious, they manage to make time to spend with family, play with their children, read, and engage in sports and recreation. To see someone rushing down the street with a takeaway cup of coffee is still unusual today. They would rather gather with friends in their cozy cafés for a small break.

The first item Babe bought for Judy was a Bodum French press coffeemaker, to encourage her to invite people to the little cottage at Tutukaka. Before Judy returned on the first anniversary of the collision, Babe and Ian carpeted and painted the cottage, and put up a little canopy to make it even more hospitable. They also readied her car, to give her the opportunity to go visiting in Whangarei. Judy was to benefit from the sensibilities of New Zealand in so many ways.

While Judy was still in the hospital recuperating—before she knew any New Zealanders, before she knew the impact the country would have on her healing—she asked Isabelle, her social worker and sometime confidante, to sneak her out the back stairwell for a little distraction. Isabelle told Judy that unfortunately she was unavailable; she was meeting some friends for a regularly scheduled Pizza Night.

"Can I come with you?" Judy remembers asking. "I haven't had pizza for three years."

"Well, this is a support group of sorts," Isabelle replied.

She explained to Judy that she met informally every month with Jigs Bradley, her supervisor, and Val Boag, the clinical leader for relationship services, to talk about their difficult cases.

"I'm a difficult case. Can I come?" Judy replied.

Isabelle did ask the other two, and Val Boag recalls that she was the most reluctant. She had not met Judy, but looking back, Val said, "I probably snorted, 'Typical American, so up-front, just wants pizza! She can come once.'"

Judy arrived with Isabelle, but tired easily and didn't say much, so they were all surprised when she wanted to know the date of the next Pizza Night.

By the time the next Pizza Night came around, Judy was living in Tutukaka, and with Babe's help, she hosted it. The five women laughed together and wept together and ate their pizza with lumps in their throats. Since the group had already evolved into something more than a clinical health care support gathering, Babe asked if she could include her friend Judy Dempster at the next Pizza Night. The original three realized that by bringing Judy Sleavin in, they had lost control of the group's original impetus. They also realized that something more significant was happening. Judy Dempster offered to change her name to Jemma, so that no one would be confused, and they all changed their names. They called themselves the Wild Girls.

When Judy Sleavin returned from the United States for the first anniversary of the collision, she brought everyone in the group floral caftans and fishnet stockings. The mischief had begun, and Judy had met her match in these women. They never abandoned their time for tears and practical advice and emotional support, but for balance they instituted the Outrageous Award. Each person attempted to win it by doing some thing excessively unconventional between meeting times, and the competitive stories every month brought raucous hilarity. Privately, the Wild Girls talked about the astounding fact that it was Judy, with her tremendous tragedy, who had injected the wackiness. Val asked, "Is this the person, or is this an American, or is this the result of her head injury?"

It wasn't always easy for Judy to be around people, even the Wild Girls. In her everyday life she continued to have uncontrollable crying spells, trouble learning new things, and difficulty remembering appointments. The flashbacks hadn't magically evaporated when she returned to New Zealand, as she had hoped. Sometimes, with conversation swirling around, she would slide right into her past. She would pull herself back out by silently thinking of the steps in her chocolate chip cookie recipe. Sometimes she had to double and triple the ingredients before she regained her composure. Any one of those flashbacks might have turned Judy into a recluse, but she fought against it. She had always taken pleasure in social activities and in cultivating friendships. She accepted every invitation to go walking or touring or quilting. She knew that some people might be reluctant to include her when she was in mourning, or even be offended by observing her hour of happiness, but it was vital to her. She wasn't trying to replace her family or immediately create new memories, but she looked forward to any outing; it gave her hope that someday she could again be a part of a community. And intuitively she knew what the author Amy Tan so eloquently said in an interview: "Hope is the adrenaline of the soul." She told me she thought if she acted like a happy person, maybe one day she would be happy again. In response to my letters asking how she was doing, she would say, "Still practicing." That had been her motivation in hosting the second Pizza Night, but even she didn't realize then that the Wild Girls would have the most profound effect on her happiness in the years to come.

In a letter to Tim dated February 1997, Judy wrote:

*I'm tired, I'm depressed, around every corner is another nightmare. I'm crying a lot more. But . . . then there's the Wild Girls and I forget my misery.*

They would become her surrogate family, her champions, her safe place. They were so tender with her, but not with the usual restraints. They offered compassion laced with honesty, respect with expectations. They invited her to be a part of their family weddings and celebrations, and they lit candles with her each year at the anniversary of the collision. They traveled to the United States as a group, to integrate her Kiwi and California families, to Italy for a cultural infusion, and to Deep Water Cove to give gratitude. They went to a jazz festival in the Bay of Islands and to a coroner's inquest in Kaikohe. They were with her for everything.

There is a large supporting cast of characters who remain interested in Judy's welfare. When I flew to New Zealand to do research and interviews for this book, I had no idea just how many people still wanted to protect her from a prying stranger's questions. These were the people involved in the search for the *Melinda Lee* or at Deep Water Cove, people involved in recovery efforts, people from the hospital, and generally people with whom Judy has had no contact for a few years now. I had to climb up on scaffolding at a construction site to seek out one reluctant individual, in order to assure him that I meant no harm to Judy. Sometimes I brought a Wild Girl or two to prop up my credentials. And when I said enough to let people know that this book was being written at Judy's request, the information flowed. They were all modest in recounting their personal involvement and efforts, but there was no reticence. The event had had effects on their own lives, and each person asked me if Judy would want to get together for a cup of coffee sometime, "whenever she felt like it."

Fortunately, I didn't have to start from scratch. Besides all the formal legal documents and reports I had access to, Annique Goldenberg had kindly produced her Hole in the Net log, with its wealth of information. Annique and Marco were on their boat, *Ruquca*, in Thailand when I contacted them, but they traveled back to New Zealand several times to see Judy and other friends they had acquired during their stay. After Judy was rescued, they were among the first to travel from Opua to Whangarei to visit her at the hospital. One day they pulled Isabelle aside and gave her some distressing news. Their daughter Geneva, then age four, had been diagnosed with leukemia. They had to leave for treatments in Auckland, and wouldn't be able to continue their usual hospital visits with Judy. Could Isabelle cover for them? they asked. They preferred that Judy think them neglectful rather than have her worried about Geneva. Isabelle was impressed that their first consideration was to shield Judy from further painful information.

Before the Goldenbergs left for Auckland, Annique urged another cruiser, Kerry Rauber, to go and visit with Judy. Kerry had an unusual story to tell. When Kerry arrived at the hospital, Isabelle said she "looked a mess." She told Isabelle she had come to see Judy, but she wondered if it would be a good thing. She wasn't even sure if Judy would remember her; they didn't know each other extremely well.

Kerry and Peter Rauber had sailed out of Bristol, England, in 1993. They met the Sleavins first in the Panama Canal, where they were rafted up together for a few hours, and then again much later, in Niue, in the South Pacific. They didn't see the family in Tonga, but they, too, departed from Nuku'alofa, some twenty-four hours after the *Melinda Lee*.

Kerry told Isabelle that she had been having visions ever since the collision. She could see Annie in red clothing, her body resting peacefully near a cluster of islands, but she couldn't find the islands on any of her charts. Isabelle was not disbelieving. Kerry seemed to know more than any of the other cruisers who had visited, and she even confirmed some of the things Judy had told Isabelle privately. But Kerry was having trouble sleeping, because of those visions and because she could "hear" Mike telling her to go visit Judy. Isabelle assured Kerry that she would arrange a meeting later, when Judy was discharged from the hospital. Kerry told her not to rush, that she and her husband, Peter, had decided to remain in New Zealand for a year to make sure Judy was going to be all right. Minutes before, Kerry had remarked to Isabelle that she and her husband didn't know the Sleavins very well, and here she was telling her they were going to remain in New Zealand to make certain of Judy's well-being. It amazed Isabelle, all these exceptional cruising folks who wanted nothing more than to improve Judy's life, whatever the adjustment to their own plans.

From the time she was a child, Kerry had to accept what she

called her "special feelings." There were times when she could see, in her mind's eye, circumstances and details that were very real to her but unknown to anyone else. They became more significant to Kerry in her teens; she would hear in the news a story of a murder, for instance, and in a momentary flash she could see some relevant information such as clothing, location of the body, and other details. Very often these details would be confirmed in later news broadcasts. She wasn't frightened, but she was a teenager and didn't want to be odd, so she tried to ignore these experiences.

When she and her husband were sailing toward Opua, New Zealand, an unusual feeling of dread came over her. Kerry sat in the cockpit, trying to understand what was occurring, and then announced to Peter that "something evil" was going to happen. As she heard herself speak, she could hardly believe the words coming from her. Her stomach was in knots. She tried to remain calm and allow thoughts to flood through her. She knew an accident would happen, to a family, and only one adult would survive. Images kept coming, and she started sketching as fast as they came. She saw a large, dark ship and felt "something sinister." She saw lights in windows, and silhouetted figures looking out. She felt very low in the water in comparison with the silhouetted images. Most of all, she felt an incredible sense of loss and desperation.

The next day, the *Melinda Lee* didn't check in on the Hole in the Net as scheduled. When *Aquavit* came on from Opua Harbour to say they had not arrived, there was a lot of speculation among the yachties on the radio. The *Melinda Lee* was never overdue, everyone agreed. Maybe they had taken shelter from the rough conditions? Someone who knew them said they were experienced enough to sail through any conditions, and would follow regulations that prohibited anchoring prior to clearing customs and immigration. Maybe they were having battery troubles? Kerry knew what had happened to them. She also knew that Annie and Ben must be dead, but she wasn't certain at that moment if it was Mike or Judy who had survived. She was certain that only one of them would come through.

She and Peter got out a detailed chart of the coast. Kerry marked a spot where the survivor could be found. Peter was skeptical. How could they call on the radio and say, "Oh, try having a look for the survivor of a collision at these coordinates"? At that point, there hadn't even been confirmation of an incident.

On the morning after the collision, Kerry was drained and shattered, but the seas were calmer in the area where they were sailing, and Peter put on the engine and slowed the boat down. He saw how distressed Kerry was, and told her they would start circling the area and look for any signs of what she had "seen." She began crying, and described to her husband a vision of Annie, in the water floating facedown, dark wavy hair tangled around her head. Kerry could "see" that she was wearing something red, and she could "see" other things caught up on the water near Annie's body. Kerry knew Annie wasn't far from them. As Peter and Kerry continued to circle, they came across flotsam. They saw cockpit cushions and various pieces of white fabric. They saw fuel cans. They also saw dolphins. Despite their best efforts, they couldn't find Annie and finally motored on into Opua. Kerry felt a sense of having deserted Annie, but she knew it would have been a recovery effort, not a rescue.

In Opua, everything was confirmed. When asked later how she could know such things, Kerry answered rhetorically.

"How do I do that? How do you explain being spoken to by a dead person? The easiest way to explain is to try to recall a recent conversation you have had with someone. You can hear their words and see their expressions, but they are not there. That is how it feels to me. I cannot reply, but I can stop it and start it. I didn't know Judy well enough to take my 'odd' experiences to her in the hospital, but I knew I had to speak to someone."

Kerry had to decide what to do with the information she had. That was when she first "heard" Mike Sleavin suggesting she take her sketches of the ship and the coordinates of the flotsam to the investigators. She contacted the New Zealand MSA and told them what she knew. The meeting did not go well.

Kerry continued to have images of Mike long after she spoke with the investigators upon her arrival in Opua, and that is when Annique suggested she speak with Isabelle. In February, when Isabelle felt Judy had recovered enough to speak with Kerry, she telephoned the cottage.

"Are you sitting down?" Isabelle recalls asking Judy. "This is going to be a difficult conversation."

Judy immediately invited Kerry to come and visit her in Tutu-kaka. Kerry's visualizations of the incident and of Annie might not have made a big difference to the investigators, but they made a huge difference to Judy. She wanted to share her own wide-awake dreams of the family, and Kerry's revelations gave her some solace, letting her know her family's presence was strong, even to comparative strangers.

On her visit, Kerry recalls being shocked that Judy remembered who she was.

"How could I forget?" Judy had said to her. "You told everyone we had wonderful children."

"It's true," Kerry had assured Judy. "Cruising kids seem much better behaved and more responsible and respectful than land kids, in general. You and Mike had great parenting skills, I could easily tell. Both your kids were wonderful, but there was something about Ben and his behavior that touched me deeply. I am so very sorry, Judy."

They were both weeping.

"You know what, Kerry?" Judy had said. "You touched my children deeply. You told so many cruisers how wonderful they were, and it got back to them, and they were so proud."

They went over to the house to see Babe, and she invited them out on the deck for tea.

"What are those islands, Babe?" Kerry recalls asking.

"The Poor Knights. A marine reserve. Subtropical currents from the north wash past and bring plankton that support coral and marine life. There are caves, as well, so it's a great dive spot," Babe said.

Kerry was still staring out. Babe continued.

"The larger, northern one is Tawhiti Rahi, and its southern partner is Aorangi Island, I believe. But from this distance, can you make out how the rocky contour looks like the knight's head? Captain Cook gave the islands the English name. If you come around a bit you can see a third island. When the sun is setting, it's a beautiful scene," Babe said.

"That's where Annie is," Kerry said quietly. "It's exactly what I saw in my mind but couldn't find on the chart."

In the years since, Judy has moved to her own place, but Babe and Ian planted three pohutakawa trees on their property, and Ian built a bench for Judy, all on a hill overlooking the ocean and the Poor Knights.

Over the course of my e-mails with Kerry, I began to worry about how disclosing those visions would affect her.

"Are you certain, Kerry? I don't want to disturb your own life with this telling," I wrote, several times.

"Does Judy want this? That's my only concern. I'll take the responsibility for the scrutiny it may bring," Kerry replied.

"I found a letter Judy wrote to her friend Tim the day after she talked with you. Every single thing you told her she repeated to Tim. You affected her deeply. She was and is so grateful to you," I said.

"Put in anything that will make Judy happy," Kerry replied.

I had also been e-mailing Sergeant Dave Palmer, the Whangarei police officer in charge of the mission to search for the *Melinda Lee*. He had been very cooperative about answering all my questions, but after several e-mails I was quite confused. He had mentioned two people sitting or standing by the dinghy, and since I knew Judy was totally alone in Deep Water Cove, I asked if he meant the fishermen who arrived later. "No, no, we called the fishermen to come in when we couldn't get closer because of the weather and the power cable," he replied in his next e-mail. I e-mailed back and asked if I could meet with him in person on my next trip to New Zealand. Perhaps I wasn't the one who was confused; perhaps it was the sergeant, I thought.

I'm glad I met him in person. There's something about Dave Palmer that lends a sense of trust and reliability. I would want him on my side in any police matter. He's also straightforward and thorough; he recalled everything down to the minute. I told him I was pleasantly surprised at his recall and articulateness. I explained my confusion at his mention of two people; it had muddled me up.

"So who were these two?" I finally asked.

"Her guardian angels," Dave replied promptly. "And I saw them from the Cessna. I put it down to eyestrain in the formal report, but I saw them. They're what caught my attention. In that weather, with those high winds, we were on a recovery mission—a recovery of bodies and salvage. No one could have survived. We expected to find the boat smashed up against the rocks of the headland of Cape Brett, perhaps."

"I knew she was fortunate to have northeasterly winds," I said.

"Yes," Dave agreed. "The prevailing westerly winds would have sent Judy on a route farther and farther out to sea; the northeasterlies blew her into land. But instead of smashing her against those unwelcoming rocks, the current obligingly pushed the dinghy around the headland into protected waters. Judy lived because her guardian angels were guiding her in."

"I believe you, Dave, and I'll share this with Judy. Thank you for telling me. But do you want this part off the record? What about your credibility with your police colleagues? Do you prefer that I leave this out?" I asked.

"I'm a Christian man, Hester, and I'm completely convinced. I had to omit it from the official report, of course, but you can leave it in the book. I'm secure in what I saw."

I told him about Kerry Rauber, with her vision of the collision and finding debris, sketching a diagram, and most of all seeing Annie. He was not surprised.

"I know Judy must have an iron will to have made it, and I

respect all that she did to survive, but sometimes we get help," Dave said. "The whole thing made a big impression on me. In the hundreds of search-and-rescue missions I've been involved in, I never before have followed up to see how the victim was doing. But in Judy's case, I went to the hospital."

Judy also made a big impression on Steve Simpson, one of the helicopter pilots, and he, too, went to see Judy at the hospital with his wife. They had children of a similar age, and the collision's aftermath had a major impact on them both. He made a career change, with the support of his wife, because after all, "what were we waiting for?" When it became known that Judy had told her story, in detail, to the helicopter personnel, Steve was offered a huge sum of money by a magazine to repeat those details. He refused.

"It's not my story," Steve said.

In New Zealand, Judy began to envision a life for herself. She knew it wouldn't be easy, but it would be easier than in the United States. The pace was too fast back home. With the imprint of the collision on her skull, her spine, and her psyche, she was certainly impaired. She was frustrated that she could no longer juggle ten tasks at a time, and even with her abundance of willpower and persistence, she realized she might never again be able to do so. But from the beginning, she had expectations of herself, and continued to add them to her daily lists.

She set up a studio for quilting and creative arts, first at Ian's Natural Wood Creations, and later at a bush-clad quarry site, Northland Craft Trust. Working with artists and craftspeople slowed down her heart rate. Still, the second year was worse than the first. She didn't have the distractions or rounds of numerous medical appointments. She wasn't traveling from the hospital in Whangarei to Tutukaka to Los Angeles to Tacoma to San Francisco, and then back to New Zealand. She didn't have "adult supervision." She wasn't cloaked in shock. The second year she had become aware of not only the magnitude but also the permanence of her loss.

*April 28, 1997*

*Dr. _____ not impressed with me. Put me back on the maximum dosage of meds. He basically said I look terrible and I've lost more weight. Oh well, gotta get myself in a better mood, got the first Swing Dance Class tonight. I'll go to the gym first and treadmill off this stress.*

At least in New Zealand, the variation in language, driving on the other side of the road, or learning to whip up a good pavlova kept her engaged and attentive. More important, in New Zealand she had no history or traditions of her own. She could walk down new paths without any reminders of her family, following in the footprints of kindly strangers who made every effort to give her a sense of belonging.

It was August 1997, and the civil suit was delayed by yet another motion from the defendants. Judy's attorneys had urged her to return to California, but she was depressed and anxious about the lawsuit, and wanted to be in Tutukaka. She begged for a reprieve, and promised to communicate by fax and telephone. She enjoyed the physical rehabilitation at the gym in Whangarei and received a lot of encouragement there. She wanted to remain in New Zealand at least until the second anniversary of the collision.

Judy loved her workouts and physiotherapy at the gym, although she was aware that the trainers were sometimes exasperated when she forgot the routines from one day to the next. The gym was where she listened to music and gave her thoughts a rest. The gym was where she saw some progress in healing her injured body. One day she noticed a stranger, an Asian man in a suit, watching her. It was unusual for anyone to be in a suit at the gym, and he definitely wasn't working out, just watching. Judy asked at the desk, but no, the staff didn't know him. He had just come in and purchased a visitor's membership for a month.

Judy, who was used to having her identity protected, was shaken. Only one time, when she was coming out of a supply store, had someone pointed and said, "That's her. The lady from the collision." Sometimes, when she was engaged in a business transaction at the bank or the grocery store, the teller or the clerk would quietly add, "We're so glad you're here," or "It's nice that you've remained with us." She always felt safe, and she had slipped into complacency. But she still couldn't understand the man's presence at the gym.

Judy rushed back to the cottage and called her attorney in San Francisco. He wasn't surprised she was being watched. He told her it may have been going on for quite some time. She asked him, "Why would they do that?"

"They might simply be gathering information about you, about your physical and emotional status, your activities," he said. He wasn't concerned they would physically harm her, but he did not want her harassed, and they discussed protection orders.

Judy told her psychiatrist in Whangarei that she was being

stalked. She asked him if he thought she was becoming more aware of life around her, or if they were becoming more blatant.

"It's possible it's deliberate, Judith. They want to cause you distress and tip the emotional balance, so you won't pursue action against them. You can't avoid them in a small town. You have to leave. They will succeed in unbalancing you in short order."

"But my lawyer has told me not to return to the United States, either. He has asked for a restraining order, but feels that I'll be vulnerable until the next step in the legal process. He wants me to go somewhere neutral, but where?"

"Try to have some family or friends meet you overseas. But leave, Judith."

She was able to make suitable arrangements, but Judy was distraught that she had to leave New Zealand. How could she not love a country that showed her the face of empathy? One newspaper columnist, summarizing the outpouring of feelings of many New Zealanders during the investigation, ended a piece with, "You are not alone. We feel your pain. We will try to find those who hurt you."

It was a stunning lack of humanity on the part of the shipping company. The ship had rammed her and abandoned her, and now agents of those who had hurt her had come ashore. Shadowing her could easily unravel Judy's hard-fought but fragile emotional stability. Conceivably, this might shut down her desire for litigation. She had to leave her refuge, Aotearoa, the land of the long white cloud.

*Twenty*

# Trials and Mediations

THE MEDIATION PROCESS LEADING UP TO A TRIAL WAS just as protracted as the South Korean investigation, but the Pan Ocean Shipping Company had not counted on Judy's stubborn and prideful nature.

Judy, on the other hand, did not realize the impact post-traumatic stress disorder would have on her attentiveness as she dealt with endless motions, depositions, appeals, and delays. Her fury at having to be the one to seek justice, after all the evidence proved her case, mobilized her throughout the proceedings. It was a turbulent and wretched time for her.

Initially, Tim Rooney sat with Judy through many of her meetings with the attorneys, where she became easily agitated. He offered her support and advice, and she trusted him implicitly. But he was unraveling, too. He had so carefully tended to Judy at his house day and night, and had resisted thinking about his own sense of loss, but his depression was resurfacing.

Mike's brother John stepped in to take Tim's place. Judy's prodigious memory gave her the ability to repeat all the details, even when her heart wasn't in it, and John Sleavin helped Judy consciously maintain some level of detachment during the particularly bleak periods. One of those bleak reckonings occurred when her attorney declared that Judy would have to decide on a monetary figure.

"What amount exactly could compensate? They've taken away my family, and they have taken away all my dreams for my family."

Revenge and justice are not opposite sides of the same coin. Judy had no interest in revenge. Here is what she was fighting for: An apology. A review and revision of procedures on the *Pan Grace*. More accountability by Pan Ocean Shipping Company. The attention of Pan Ocean's third-tier insurance company, Lloyd's of London, so they would have stringent requirements before they would underwrite policies. Monetary funds to provide a legacy for her family in the form of a foundation to promote safety at sea for all mariners. Monetary funds to pay her legal fees and her medical bills.

Here is what she really wanted: Mike, Ben, and Annie.

On August 27, 1996, plaintiff Judith Sleavin filed her complaint in the United States District Court for the Northern District of California. The complaint alleged the following causes of action: maritime negligence, negligent infliction of emotional distress, intentional infliction of emotional distress, intentional failure to rescue, negligent failure to rescue, wrongful death, pre-death pain and suffering, and property damage.

Depositions of the crew members of the *Pan Grace* were

taken over a ten-day period in November 1996 in Seoul, and Judy's deposition was taken over a three-day period in December 1996 in San Francisco.

*The attorneys for the Pan Ocean Shipping Company asked for a mediation, and then another.* Nothing was accomplished; their offers to settle the case amounted to a sum that would not even cover Judy's expenses. She returned to New Zealand after the mediation sessions to regain her strength. She wrote to her attorney, telling him she would not pay for another mediation until something reasonable to negotiate was presented in writing by the defendants. She added that the initial two meetings were not a waste of time: they had given Judy the opportunity to understand that Pan Ocean was willing to use tactics to interrupt, postpone, and suspend proceedings, in an attempt to wear her down.

*The defendants filed several motions to have the case dismissed,* on the basis that the *Melinda Lee* was an unseaworthy vessel, and that its crew, not the crew of *Pan Grace,* was to blame for any alleged collision or injuries. Judy's attorney filed arguments in return, pointing out the findings of blame attributed to the *Pan Grace* by the South Korean authorities. The defendants' motions to dismiss were denied.

*The defendants filed a motion to have the venue changed to a Korean court.* A trial in South Korea would be Pan Ocean's last opportunity to exert political control over the proceedings. Judy's attorneys produced affidavits from the psychiatrists who had evaluated or treated her. They all agreed that she would come to a harmful emotional state if the venue were changed. In Judy's affidavit, she said, in part, "I feel totally incapable of participating in a proceeding in Korea. I do not speak or understand the language. The anger and resentment I feel toward Pan Ocean and its employees are beyond description." Eventually that motion was denied.

*The defendants filed a motion to exclude all punitive damages under the Death on the High Seas Act (DOHSA).* This would reduce the amount of money awarded to a mere fraction of what Judy had asked. That motion was granted. The United States District Court held that such damages were not recoverable under maritime law, and the defendants' motion should prevail. The Circuit Court of Appeals refused to hear an interlocutory appeal of this issue.

In 1920 the United States Congress passed the Death on the High Seas Act. "Whenever the death of a person shall be caused by wrongful act, neglect, or default occurring on the high seas beyond a marine league [three nautical miles] from the shore of any state, or the District of Columbia, or the territories or dependencies of the United States, the representative may maintain a suit for damages."

It appeared to be a forward-thinking act, and in 1920 it most likely was. It made it easier for the widows of merchant seamen to recover what the "breadwinner" would have earned for the rest of his working life, when death occurred in international waters. Damages are confined to pecuniary (economic) damages only, and DOHSA does not allow for punitive damages, also known as exemplary damages. Punitive damages are a sort of punishment intended to discourage a defendant and are usually awarded when the defendant has done something destructive. Even if the circumstance of a seaman's death was due to a wrongful act or the employer's neglect, DOHSA did not allow punitive damages to be brought against an at-fault party in international waters.

To be clear, then, the Death on the High Seas Act is still in effect and was relevant to Judy's civil suit. She was confined to seeking pecuniary damages only: the projected future earnings of Mike and the fair market value of the *Melinda Lee*. Her children were not wage earners; their lives were worth nothing according to DOHSA. It also did not allow for recovery for the grief, mental anguish, pre-death pain and suffering, and loss of love and companionship. The defendants also argued that, according to DOHSA, the *Melinda Lee* crew contributed to the accident (contributory negligence). Therefore her pecuniary award "may be reduced accordingly."

Judy was determined to fund a foundation that would support international maritime safety, and she fought on, despite the fact that her recoverable damages would be limited. Her attorney fought on as well, determined to include compensation for intentional failure to rescue, negligent failure to rescue, and wrongful death. Judy was well represented by him; he was an experienced and skillful maritime attorney, and passionate about her story and her welfare. He was simply heavily restricted by DOHSA.

No one could have expected that a piece of legislation from 1920, which limits amendment remedies and does not take into account the realities of modern-day travel, could affect not only recreational boaters but airline and cruise ship passengers, too, whenever they venture one marine league, or three nautical miles, from United States shores.

The families of passengers aboard a Trans World Airlines flight learned about the restrictions of the Death on the High Seas Act in 1996. TWA Flight 800, a Boeing 747 bound from New York to Paris, exploded minutes from takeoff and plunged into the sea nine miles off Long Island Sound, on July 17, 1996. All 230 people aboard were killed. Their relatives discovered that DOHSA applied to aviation accidents beyond the three-nautical-mile limit and did not allow punitive damages to be brought against the airline or the manufacturer. Included in the passenger list were sixteen members of a high school French club. The families of the students, and of any other children aboard, learned they could be deprived of any compensation other than funeral expenses. Their children, like Ben and Annie, were not wage earners, and their parents could assert little actual pecuniary loss with their deaths.

Relatives of the passengers from the TWA crash contacted their senators; the impetus for congressional hearings in 1997 to amend DOHSA came from this aviation disaster. Judy was still doing battle, and there was hope her case could be expanded to include punitive damages. But the Senate did not pass the amendment after those hearings. The bill languished in the Senate Commerce Committee, and ironically it was a senator from Mike's home state of Washington, Slade Gorton, who strongly opposed any changes; after all, Washington was also the home of Boeing.

By contrast, Senator Ron Wyden of Oregon had been deeply affected by the devastating circumstances of the story when

John Sleavin, hoping for a United States presence in the investigation, had first written to him. Senator Wyden had remained interested in the outcome. He contacted John and suggested that John speak before the next Senate hearing on DOHSA, scheduled for April 1998. Judy's trial was scheduled for May of that year.

It was the end of November 1997. Judy had just returned to New Zealand for the second anniversary of the collision. She received a call from her attorney in San Francisco. He told her he had just been informed that the defendants had subpoenaed her medical and psychiatric records.

"But my psychiatrist in Seattle told me that she wasn't taking notes, in case of litigation."

He asked what could be in the notes. Judy told him that she couldn't remember specifically, but that she had not concealed any of her feelings. She might have talked about family and friends, venting about petty things that irked her, as a substitute for the rage over the *Pan Grace* and the sorrow over Mike, Ben, and Annie. He told her everything could be used, and perhaps she might want to ask family and friends to stay away from the trial.

"Do you mean to say that they're going to do their best to remove absolutely everybody from my life, until I have no emotional support whatsoever?" she asked in disbelief.

With that as leverage, another mediation session was scheduled for January 1998. Judy had wanted to wait until May for the trial, since John Sleavin would be testifying before the Senate in April. She totally trusted John and knew him extremely well; he and his wife, Kathi, had taken her on their honeymoon in France when she had to flee New Zealand after noticing her stalker.

John accompanied Judy to the mediation in January. At an earlier mediation she had been offered an annuity, but she had made it very clear that she was interested only in a lump sum, which she would need to fund her future maritime safety foundation. Despite this, the entire first day was spent with a representative hired to talk about annuities. Judy was ready to leave. John reassured her it was only a method of wearing her down for the next day. He told Judy that, after viewing all her medical records, they would be aware of her vulnerabilities: her lack of concentration skills, her anxiety and hypervigilance in unfamiliar surroundings. They had purposely scheduled the mediation in a small, windowless room where she would feel confined and helpless.

The second day the approach was similar, and the amount of money offered was far from what she should reasonably expect. Among the pressures brought to bear were excerpts from her counseling sessions. Predictably, as the mediation progressed, Judy fell apart.

"I'm done, I'm done!" John remembers her crying. "What more do you want from me?"

Judy got up to leave, and John rose with her. The mediator realized this was not some tactic, that she was indeed "done." He promised he would bring the mediation to a successful conclusion within the hour.

On January 9, 1998, in the county of San Francisco in the State of California, Judy settled with the Pan Ocean Shipping Company, discharging them from any further actions related to the deaths of her family and her personal injuries. The Pan Ocean Shipping Company never apologized.

On April 22, 1998, John Sleavin testified before the Senate Commerce Committee. It was too late to benefit Judy, he knew; he was there to represent all future maritime victims. By all accounts his testimony was riveting. Several committee members offered emotional condolences and sincere thanks for John's participation, but no changes were made to the Act.

Another aviation accident brought the consequences of DOHSA to light again. A Swissair plane, bound from New York to Geneva, crashed five miles off the coast of Nova Scotia, and all 229 people aboard were killed. Two years later, the United States Congress passed an amended version of the Death on the High Seas Act into law. It was still restrictive, but "loss of care, comfort and companionship" were added to recoverable damages. Senator Ron Wyden had remained fervent in his support of the Sleavin family's cause, but the amendment applies only to aviation accidents. Maritime casualties are not included.

But, cruise ships are not immune to catastrophic accidents. There have been collisions, fires on board, groundings, and even a pirate attack one hundred miles off the coast of Somalia. Someday there could be a significant disaster. Cruise ships may carry as many as three thousand passengers, many of whom are retirees; as non–active wage earners, they would have the same burden as children to prove any pecuniary damage.

Excluding any concern with the effects that DOHSA would have in a maritime catastrophe, complicated ownership arrangements and flag-of-convenience ship registration—widespread among the cruise industry—have created extreme uncertainty over accountability in any incidents.

Judy called me immediately after the final mediation. She wondered if I could fly to California. When we met, she was happy to see me but distressed.

"I threw in the towel," she said.

I told her I admired her strength of purpose.

"The psychiatrist told me she wouldn't take notes, in case of litigation, but there they were, with quotation marks around my comments! I couldn't afford to lose anyone else, and who knows how I might have vented?"

Later, I made every effort to learn how such a standard of medical ethics could be breached, but to no avail.

At the time, I told Judy I thought she had behaved courageously in such a stressful situation. She was not consoled. She reiterated that she wanted to have a foundation with a global impact. She wanted to establish shipping lanes near busy harbors in countries where they didn't exist. She wanted to dredge out narrow channels. She wanted to set up schools to train future maritime crews in nations where the education wasn't offered. She wanted to inform recreational boaters how to be meticulously prepared.

"I promised I'd help," I said, "and we can start a foundation that will have an impact, one small program at a time."

In 1999, Judy, Maureen Lull, and I set up the Sleavin Family Foundation, funded by Judy. Maureen and I were just as passionate as Judy. Maureen elected to give up most of her civil engineering projects, and I resigned from my position at the University of Washington. We vowed that in the names of Mike, Ben, and Annie, we would do everything in our power to learn, educate, and inform, so that no one would ever have to die as they did, and no one would ever have to suffer as Judy did. Judy helped behind the scenes as we set up presentations, consulted on safety issues, wrote articles, and researched new equipment. We met with shipping executives and Coast Guard personnel who encouraged and supported our mission, and provided us with perspective and crucial data. We learned from and shared information with conscientious and talented recreational boaters in yacht clubs and power squadrons who meticulously prepared for a daysail or a race or a motoring holiday. We learned from and shared information with accomplished and exceptional offshore sailors. We gained indispensable understanding from scrupulous and diligent professional mariners, and collaborated with them to set up cooperative programs that would begin to build a maritime community and support safety at sea for everyone. Judy knew she could never reconstruct her old life, but it helped her to know that she might save the lives of others.

*Twenty-one*

# Reflections

✸

WHAT KIND OF TRAVEL STORIES DO YOU TELL ABOUT yourself when all the main characters are gone? If your story is not only exotic but exceptional and terrifying, you have the opportunity to tell a public tale. Judy certainly was inundated with offers: authors, filmmakers, documentarians, and newspapers from all over the world made requests. Interest was high, and often sympathetic. A filmmaker in Quebec presented the idea of having his sister, a nurse, sit with Judy throughout the making of a documentary he wished to produce for the Canadian Broadcasting Corporation. But Judy refused every offer. She didn't want to be the next tragedy of the week, an expression given to misfortunes that become well known and then are tossed aside. Other than a short, gracious memo she sent to one of the popular television shows in Auckland, Judy remained silent, and all the details went untold. She needed to form a new identity before she became the story itself in everyone's eyes. Whenever she asked my advice about going public, I told her she would know when the timing was right. For me, she already had her new identity. She was the only real mermaid I would ever know, mysteriously arising out of the sea, wounded, to transform herself over and over again.

Judy is not uncomplicated. She has no filter when it comes to sharing gossip with her Wild Girls, such as the Internet dating habits of widows. She dishes up her daily interpersonal dramas, mostly for their entertainment value.

It is the details withheld, the ones Judy suppresses, that are essential to those who want to help her manage her life. When I ask Judy why she doesn't tell these cherished friends that it takes her two days of crying to recover from the visits with their children, she just shakes her head.

"The Wild Girls tell me that it hits them in the heart when you're so loving toward their kids. But they want to look out for you as well. Some information about your emotional state would help them figure out ways to support you," I suggest.

"I can't tell them. I don't want to be left out of anything," she replies.

Judy is more practical than philosophical, buoyed more by self-determination and accomplishment than by self-reflection. I think this is what saved her. She records more than she interprets, and this allows her to stay in the moment rather than worry and dissect the consequences or ramifications of things that happen. Out there, alone, on top of a partially inflated dinghy, in huge seas, ravaged and battered by the deaths of her loved ones, she took on the tasks at hand and waited to ask the big question "Why?" until after she was safely rescued. "Why?" wouldn't have helped, and the mind trips taken in any introspective moments might have taken her farther out to sea.

———

In September 2000, John and I sailed to Hawaii. I wasn't particularly happy on that passage. We had bought a bigger, but older, fiberglass sailboat that needed a lot of modification, and it had been out of the water more than in. I wasn't accustomed to the systems on the boat. We, too, were older and more vulnerable to fatigue in all those hours of vigilant watchkeeping. And we had terrible weather. The wind blew, and the seas got larger and larger, big rollers practically swamping us from behind.

Sailing downwind in high winds, surfing big waves, it is difficult to steer a straight course. This leaves you vulnerable to the danger of an accidental jibe, because any small shift in course can result in the wind getting behind the mainsail and pushing the sail to the other side of the boat. The danger comes from the main boom, because there is the risk of someone being injured or even knocked overboard as it swings across the center of the boat uncontrollably. We had a huge wooden boom, and I knew that someday, if I wasn't careful, an accidental jibe would knock me right across the International Dateline. I studied those big seas and checked the jibe preventer, windvane, and the helm constantly, and I kept an anxious eye on that boom.

I hadn't considered that I might also be more fearful because of what had happened to the Sleavins, and I was let down and shaken that John was so impatient with me; it was the first time in our twenty years together that I felt we didn't mesh on a seagoing passage. When we reached Molokai and I finally got out of my foul-weather gear, I expressed my misgivings. John told me we would work together until I felt more comfortable, and he assured me that I would get acclimatized to our sea life again. As we sailed farther and farther west on our circumnavigation route, by and large I did find my pace and rhythm. We regained that easy togetherness of our long-distance sailing experiences. We even held hands underwater as we explored new reefs. I looked forward to the time when we would begin to plan our passages to Thailand and South Africa and Europe.

I recall Judy telling me how unsettled she felt for the first six months of their circumnavigation. She and Mike knew it would be necessary for them to travel the routes most frequented, because of the children. Judy wanted them to interact as often as possible with other cruising families. But Mike liked to move from spot to spot quickly and was more impatient than she to discover the next anchorage.

Schooling proved to be much more time-consuming and labor-intensive than they had expected. Ben was easily distracted, and Annie wanted to do whatever her big brother was doing. And the laundry. Everyone was sticky from the heat and gritty from saltwater showers, and there was always laundry. Forget the glossy magazines with sailors in pristine outfits clinking their frosty glasses together in a toast to the good life. At every anchorage, Judy sat on the deck with a huge bucket and an old-fashioned wringer-type washer, cleaning the salt and sweat from her family's T-shirts.

When they reached Panama, they decided on a new approach. In each country, they would secure the boat and get on the bus for land excursions and explorations. It contributed to everyone's geographical awareness, enriched the children's education, added balance to the family's cruising life, and slowed Mike down. He took over Annie's schooling, and Ben thrived on the one-on-one attention Judy was able to bring to his instruction. Mike relished the idea that the children were gaining an awareness of the simplicity with which other people lived, and both parents admired the flourishing generosity of Ben and Annie as they gave away their toys and clothes. As their travels continued, the wringer rusted out, and even doing the laundry became a family affair. They found their pace and their rhythm.

In September 2001, I was away from the boat for a month and in the United States. I had been invited to Washington, D.C., to participate on behalf of the Sleavin Family Foundation in a workshop on recreational boating engagement strategy for harbor safety, sponsored by the United States Coast Guard. I had never been to Washington, but this was going to be a quick trip, with no sightseeing involved. The meeting was to last most of the day: September 11, and I was scheduled to leave for Seattle early the following morning.

When the first plane hit the World Trade Center tower in New York at 8:46 A.M., I was in the security line at the U.S. Department of Transportation building, waiting to put my briefcase on the belt. There was a small television mounted above us, and looking at the news, we all assumed we were watching an accident. I rode the elevator up to the meeting and took my place with the other attendees. There was a facilitator, and each of us gave a short speech about our respective interest in maritime safety. I was impressed with the group, which included some high-ranking Coast Guard officials, an admiral from the Pentagon, a representative from the National Safe Boating Council, one from the U.S. Department of State, a well-known advocate for harbor safety from San Francisco, and two colleagues from the BoatU.S. Foundation. When the second plane hit the other tower at 9:03 A.M., we were unaware.

We were in the process of going around the table with introductions when the third plane slammed into the Pentagon at 9:37 A.M., and we were still unaware. But soon after, there was a knock on the door. The admiral was called out, a cell phone rang, there was some discussion in an undertone, and we were asked to go down to the underground Metro and leave the building. Someone whispered to me that something terrible must have happened. Most of the attendees lived and worked in the surrounding area and made a hasty exit; I didn't even know where I was in relation to my hotel.

I went down to the Metro; it was total chaos. People were yelling "Turn off your cell phones" and "Get going" and "Get out of here!" The whole building was evacuated; apparently they knew a fourth airplane was missing on radar, possibly headed for the White House. Someone near me shouted, "The White House is too low to be a good target. Why not a tall federal building like this one? That's why we're being evacuated!"

It was possibly around then that United Airlines Flight 93 crashed in a rural Pennsylvania field, thanks to the remarkable heroics of the passengers. We weren't aware of this occurrence in the Metro station. I was pushed onto a train going in the wrong direction. By the time I got myself sorted out and back to my hotel, there were boards covering the entrance, with one door available to get in. A guard with a clipboard permitted registered guests to enter.

The Washington, D.C., area wasn't as harrowing or heart-breaking as the New York scene, because the Pentagon isn't in the middle of the city, and there were many fewer deaths. But it was extremely sad and surreal. And it would get more so. The District of Columbia declared a state of emergency, and every-one was asked to remain inside.

I looked out the window of my hotel room, which was on the top floor, to neighboring rooftops. National Guardsmen were on those roofs, standing vigilant, with rifles. A small fighter jet flew low. The streets were bare within two hours, and would remain so. I ran between my window and the television all day. I didn't know it then, but I would be stuck there for eight more days.

At some point, I went to Dulles International Airport to make arrangements to get home. I was at the ticket counter for more than an hour, although I was the only customer. I was fortunate that my driver had waited; the airport was empty, with the exception of more National Guardsmen, and it was a long way back to the city. He asked me what had happened in there.

"Twelve hundred dollars?" He was amazed when he heard how much I had been charged for my one-way ticket. "For that amount I would have happily driven you to Seattle, and we could have left right now," he said.

His name was Alex Yamoah, and his usual customers were business executives and government personnel. With a state of emergency in effect, he had no customers, and it would have been the perfect way for me to make the cross-country trip.

When we arrived back in the city, I asked him if we could make one stop. "I'd like to see the Lincoln Memorial. Do you have time?" When we got there, he opened the car door and told me he would accompany me. It was nighttime, and there were floodlights illuminating the white monuments and young people sitting on the steps with lit candles as we walked up to the Lincoln Memorial. Alex looked very distinguished in his suit, with his hands clasped behind his back, and I'm sure many of the people holding vigil thought he was some kind of dignitary as he read parts of Lincoln's Gettysburg Address to me.

Alex was born in Ghana, I in Canada, but we both shared the horror and sorrow of the 9/11 tragedy. We couldn't embrace the enormity of what had happened only days ago, but that evening we were in the right place to contemplate hopefulness in the history here.

Much of my anxiety over those nine long days was related to Judy. I knew she was supposed to be nearby, for a bicycling trip along the Potomac River. I hadn't expected to be in Washington for the meeting, so we hadn't made any arrangements to meet. She was staying with Mike's sister Sharon, but I didn't know Sharon's married name. The only thing that stuck in my mind was that Sharon and Bill's home in Virginia was only five miles from the Pentagon. Was there some horrendous chance that Judy had actually witnessed the plane flying into the Pentagon? If so, it would have been traumatic for her beyond measure.

I found out much later that she and some of the Sleavin siblings had started out early on the morning of September 11.

They had been cycling along a trail, and stopped at a café around 9:30 A.M. As they waited for their coffee, Judy saw some of the television footage of the World Trade Center. She became hysterical. She called her mother, but Caryl had no idea what she was talking about; it was 6:30 A.M. on the West Coast, and her mother hadn't yet heard the news. Judy was too panic-stricken to make herself understood. She called and woke up a psychiatrist in California. He told her to leave immediately, to go somewhere she could feel safe. Her PTSD triggers had fired, and she was having trouble relating to the new trauma. Her old trauma came flooding back, and she was completely disoriented. The Sleavins took care of her, made all the arrangements, and in short order she was whisked away.

Judy is, or was, geopolitically well informed, but we—her family and friends—never discuss with her September 11; the tsunamis in Thailand and Sri Lanka; the flooding in Burma; the bombings in Bali, Madrid, and London; the earthquakes in Pakistan and China; or the horror of Darfur. We don't talk about the war in Iraq or Afghanistan with Judy. And we shield her from the pictures on CNN of any disasters, especially the ones with little children laid out in rows.

In September 2002, John and I were in Batnapi Village, Vanuatu. We lay in the forward berth in misery and pain. After hundreds of hours of spearfishing expeditions, and hundreds of wonderful meals from the bounty of the sea, here we had dined on a red snapper laden with ciguatera toxin. The toxin has no effect on the fish itself; nor is the toxin destroyed upon cooking. So you can't detect that a fish is full of ill will toward you until it affects almost every organ system in your body, one way or another.

Two other sailboats arrived in the anchorage on the day John speared the fish, so we were all invited to a potluck on the boat *Manati*. We shared the snapper and, unknowingly, the toxin. Terri, the only other woman in our group of six, suffered the same excruciating leg pains as I did; otherwise the toxin affected the six of us equally and considerably. Each day the chief would visit our three boats in an outrigger canoe, to make sure we were still alive. There are fatalities attributed to this toxin, but fortunately none of us succumbed.

After a month, I was able to write a group letter and let our fans know that we were still around. We received appreciative replies in response to my detailed description of the follies, and some of our friends wondered how we found such absurdity in the situation.

I got a frantic reply from Judy. She, with her great sense of humor, didn't see the humor in it at all. I called her when we arrived in New Caledonia to assure her that we were going to be fine.

"Tell me you're okay," she kept repeating. She was crying.

This was the crack in her armor; this was where her bravery ended. She knew that the absolute worst had already happened to her, but she was fearful for the rest of us in her life. And not just the ones at sea. She insists that everyone around her be healthy, safe, and happy.

I remember once expressing my concern when she headed out to meet an unknown man from the Internet, but she brushed me off. I thought it might be dangerous, but Judy told me I didn't understand. Sometime later I asked, "Were you hoping to get hurt? Were you testing yourself?"

"No, no, I wasn't trying to live on the edge; I really felt that nothing would happen to me. For a very long time after I was rescued, I felt invincible. I had never kept up with any of those athletic Sleavins before, despite my best efforts, but when I joined John and Kathi and Sharon in France for the bike trip, I took every curve at their speed," Judy said.

She told me she had promised Ben and Annie they could learn to ski their first winter in New Zealand. After the collision Judy didn't really want to go skiing because of the cold and her flashbacks, but she went anyway. Just for Ben and Annie. "I pointed my skis straight downhill for the first time in my life. I felt indestructible." She paused, reflective. "Later the cold got to me, and I was an emotional mess."

Mike and Judy were never oblivious to the way their dream would affect Ben and Annie. Every action they took reflected their concern for the children. They constantly evaluated their well-being and were prepared at any time to change course or even curtail the journey if the children didn't thrive. Everyone who visited the *Melinda Lee* remarked on how assured and confident the children were, and how astonishing it was for the four of them to be so positively engaged in one another's lives. However, a question I am asked over and over is how anyone could take children out on the high seas. I really don't want to be glib when I answer, but I point out that no one thinks twice about putting a child in an automobile. Yet statistics from the nonprofit organization Advocates for Highway and Auto Safety reveal that approximately five hundred children between the ages of five and nine die each year in the United States in auto accidents.

Judy answered endless questions as I worked on this book. She gave me every legal document and investigative report. She shared her files of letters and e-mails and her private journals with the rawest of feelings. Earlier, when it was determined that we would indeed start a foundation for maritime safety, I asked Judy if I could explore all the things the Sleavins could have done differently to avoid the collision. "Can I discuss any issue openly, even ones that might point the finger at you?" I asked.

"Go for it," she replied. "How will anyone learn from this otherwise?"

She isn't just concerned about the people she knows; she wants to extend her lessons far beyond her circle, in any way she can. Envision the mental power it took for her, with fractured and crushed vertebrae, to haul that dinghy up, high and dry, in case it might be needed for forensic evidence, and you'll understand just how determined she is in every task she undertakes. Judy is a very unusual person.

With her settlement, she bought a bach (New Zealanders' word for a simple holiday retreat) to live in as her home. Instead of indoor plumbing, it has a long drop (the term speaks for itself). She wanted to use the bulk of the money to fund programs for maritime safety and to collaborate with professional mariners, so that everyone might be included in her dream for a safer world. Judy's sense of purpose sustains her and, fortunately, often eclipses her need to make sense of what happened.

Collisions occur all over the world, often between two large vessels. We don't have an accurate picture of how often they happen, because of loose governance over offshore waters, unenforceable regulations, and, sometimes, poor standards. The *Pan Grace* was easy to trace to South Korea, and its South Korean crew was easy to locate. But this is unusual. More often there is no genuine link between flag and ship, and the crew, as one writer put it, could represent the United Nations. It seems an almost impossible task to uncover the layers and assign blame when the ship is built in one country, the owners are of a second country, the ship is registered in yet another, and the captain and crew are from five other countries. Given that vessels can be registered in flag nations that are politically disintegrating, or landlocked, or uninterested in outcomes, there is a huge general issue of accountability.

Not many of the 167 member states of the International Maritime Organization (IMO) carry out full investigations into accidents involving their vessels. Even fewer have totally independent accident investigation bodies.

The second mate made a terrible error. In a cover-up, of both the error and the abandonment, the master of the *Pan Grace* used the old Nixon tape ploy: the course recorder had a coincidental paper jam during the significant hours. The Pan Ocean Shipping Company condoned the cover-up and attempted to slant the investigation to achieve its own agenda. To their credit, however, the South Korean Maritime Authorities did carry out a full investigation, in a responsible manner. The prosecutor's decision not to indict, and the shipping company's decision not to discipline, may have been less than upright, but the maritime authorities' comprehensive inquiry and examination of the evidence was fruitful; it brought to light valuable information.

It was obvious to me from the records of some of the depositions that there were crew members on the *Pan Grace* who were knowledgeable and ethical, and who would have been more forthcoming. They must have been intimidated by company officials in the room. Each time a crew member provided any important details, a Pan Ocean official would ask for a break. When the questioning resumed, the responses would be either "I don't understand" or "I don't remember." For instance, the chief mate on the *Pan Grace* testified that at the time he relieved the second mate on November 24 at 0400, he looked at the course recorder, the same course recorder that supposedly was inoperable. Minutes later he claimed to have no memory after his testimony was interrupted by a Pan Ocean representative. There were other contradictions, but crew members were cowed into resisting further clarification. I admire those who at least made an effort to tell the truth. Nevertheless, I don't think the company officials represented their best interests. Justice is for the common good; had justice prevailed, it would have been another step in improving life for everybody.

Nations worldwide are rapidly expanding trade, and this will only increase seaborne traffic. There are certainly flag states that have commendable standards, with responsible and conscientious ownership; they operate safe, expertly run vessels. Those flag states that do not insist upon exemplary standards of seamanship, operations, and conditions for their crews are inviting further catastrophes. And if there is an unfortunate maritime casualty and the flag state is allowed to withhold evidence, or chooses not to undertake an investigation at all, then no one can learn from the errors or lapses in judgment and equipment. In contrast—perhaps because so many commercial flights carry more passengers than cargo—the aviation industry has been a model in frank discussions and candid investigations, resulting in improvements in safety standards for all of us.

My own knowledge has been greatly enhanced by the network of professional mariners who are concerned with advancing safety in our harbors and out at sea. I have a very high opinion of their educational backgrounds, intensive training, skills, and competence. Some of them spent hours providing me with resource material for my Sleavin Family Foundation work. Some accompanied me to presentations and answered questions posed by recreational boaters. And some encouraged me to get on ships in order to familiarize myself with the routines required for the safe transit of these vessels from coastal waters to inland harbors. I have met many harbor pilots and seagoing captains who are conscientious far beyond their credentials. I have met several seagoing captains who diverted their container ships to rescue sailors in storm-driven waters. I have not met a single professional mariner who would hesitate to change course to help a sailor in distress.

Weeping, I read a line in one of Judy's journals: "Why does God have to show me the face of death up close?"

"Do you still believe in God?" I asked her later.

She gave me an unqualified yes. She told me how glad she was that Kerry Rauber had shared her vision of Mike giving her messages, and of Annie at the Poor Knights. She liked that

I had recently told her about Sergeant Dave Palmer's belief that she'd had guardian angels guiding her to safety in the dinghy. "I know about God now, and I know about heaven, too," she said. "I feel more connected to the universe."

We once discussed the fact that their chosen, unconventional life had given the Sleavin family an incomparable experience of being together. Really being together. Sharing a joyful existence. "I know," Judy replied quietly. "That does give me some sense of peace. Especially since I can feel their presence so often. Ben, especially, likes to give me little tips on living."

*Twenty-Two*

# Ten Degrees of Reckoning

※

TEN DEGREES. THE SECOND MATE MADE A FATAL ERROR, based not upon calculations or technology or even experience. He became flustered as his ship was approaching the sailboat, and he had done nothing to correct his course when he had the time. So, on the basis of nothing more than panic, he quickly shouted out a maneuver to the helmsman. Ten degrees, and a family was destroyed.

Look at a protractor. The marked numbers for measuring angles are placed at 10-degree intervals. Such a small modification, with a consequence of such enormous magnitude. In all probability, many of us have had our lives altered by 10 degrees. A 10-degree turn, not necessarily made in panic, not necessarily even one we're aware of, but changing everything just the same. I am not dismissing the consequences of accidents of birth, or geography, or natural disasters, but I want to set them aside to address the consequences of smaller things—the narrow angle of 10 degrees, the single action or tiny incident—

that can change the outcome of our lives. What if we had taken a different course at school, been late for work at the World Trade Center on September 11, stepped off the curb too early, answered the phone, not answered the phone?

Even deliberative and well-reasoned alterations can have unexpected results. So we need to embrace the idea of living well, as Mike and Judy did. It is not a contradiction to live both blissfully and responsibly, or joyously and ethically, or serenely and enterprisingly.

Often I am asked if Judy really has any sense of peace, or if she is awash in anger at the injustice, or awash in the guilt of surviving. Whatever peace she has comes from feeling no regrets about the fullness with which her family lived on a daily basis. Her instincts as a wife and mother were unerring; how could her family be spoiled by her loving words, by her letting them know how cherished they were, by how joyous her time with them was? She always did the best she was capable of, and her capabilities were tremendous. Her refusal to conform helped her in making decisions that were right for her, and then for her family.

I know Judy chose to be happy very early on. After the collision, her beloved uncle Milton wrote her a letter assuring her that she would get through this ordeal. He said that as an infant in her crib, Judy learned to shake the nearby venetian blinds so that her grandmother would come in and smother her with kisses. He added that he prayed every morning and every night that Judy would remember she had always had the skill to make the most of exactly where she was at the moment.

For me, Judy is the unsurpassed example of a person eager to cultivate a sense of happiness in the present tense. None of us gets to choose how we are going to die, or when, for that matter. But each of us can take a page from Judy's book and decide how we are going to live. If Judy had not continued to reshape herself throughout her life, I doubt that she would have had the will to survive when her colossal test came about. She evolved from a fatherless child into a feisty teenager; then into an artist, a wife, an engineer; then into a mother; and then into a cruiser, a teacher, and a navigator; and finally into a widow and a childless mother. But of course, I shouldn't say "finally," because this isn't the end of her story. She has never defined herself as a victim. She will persist in reshaping herself and her life, although the permanent pain of these heartbreaking events could easily have left her powerless. There was no pivotal event when she realized she had to live; no epiphany, no big turning point. She had always challenged herself, and that helped with the process. But really, as trite as it sounds, it is still a day at a time, sometimes just a step at a time. Certainly, some days her steps falter, when the evidence of an altered life is too overwhelming. Some days, her steps are rather jaunty, leading to a skip, a more complicated step, and—on the very good days—a tango.

# Epilogue

�֎

THE YACHT *MELINDA LEE* REMAINS SUNKEN SOME twenty-five nautical miles to the north-northeast of Cape Brett, New Zealand. She is presumed to be lying at a depth of approximately 600 meters. There is nothing to distinguish the heartbreak there, except the GPS coordinates: latitude 34°47'3" south, longitude 174°25'25" east.

The dinghy, reinflated and cleaned, sits on a trailer in Judy's garage.

On Friday, December 13, 2002, at ten A.M., in the Council Chambers of Whangarei, Judy became a citizen of New Zealand. Her group of new citizens was made up of three people from England, three from India, one from Canada, one from South Korea, and one from the Philippines. Judy now divides her time between the United States and New Zealand, the spiritual home of her family.

Each November, as the cold, rainy season settles in Tacoma and the anniversary of the collision approaches, Catherine

Sleavin puts on the vest that Michael made for her with pencils instead of knitting needles and feels the warmth and love of her dearly beloved son. About Judy she says, "I dearly love her. She filled Michael, Ben, and Annie's lives with unbounded love and joy. All I want for her is happiness again."

Maureen and Richard Lull reconsidered their circumnavigation plans and sold their racing Shock 35, *Aftershock*. For water sports, Richard can pass on his impressive surfing skills to their wonderful son, born in August 1996. Judy made him his first quilt, forty blocks of tropical fish in purples, blues, and greens.

Geneva Goldenberg is a healthy, happy child, in complete remission from leukemia, still sailing with her parents, Annique and Marco, and last heard from in Malaysia. They have added a little brother as junior crew on *Ruquca*.

Kerry and Peter Rauber had a little boy in March 1998. They didn't name him Ben out of respect to Judy, but Kerry says, "I hope I am bringing up a little chap exactly like him." They and their son live happily in Switzerland, Peter's home country. Kerry still sees images of Annie resting peacefully near the Poor Knights.

John and Kathi Sleavin had a little boy. Apparently inviting Judy on their honeymoon didn't interfere with family planning. Aidan has become another one of the adventurous Sleavins; bicycling first in a BOB Trailer, he has graduated to a Third Wheel.

On November 24, 2005, ten years to the day after the collision, Tim Rooney died in his sleep, at the age of fifty-two.

Erica Crenshaw, from *Aquavit*, wrote that on her night watches she thinks of Judy as Orion, and Mike, Ben, and Annie as the three stars in Orion's Belt.

———

Judy has developed compensatory skills to make up for any visual deficits with her agnosia from the brain injury. She stays physically active—walking, bicycling, and kayaking in estuaries—to ward off any physical disability from her vertebral injuries. Occasionally she goes sailing, and while she still understands the appeal, she refers to herself now as a landlubber. She wrote a letter to Patagonia, the clothing manufacturer, thanking the company for saving her from hypothermia, and she made a donation to Northland Emergency Services Trust, which provided the helicopter and personnel for her search and rescue.

Over the years, Judy's flashbacks have mostly subsided. She still cannot concentrate if she has not made her daily lists or if she is under stress. She completes jigsaw puzzles and plays computer games to improve those concentration skills. She has meltdowns about once a month, and more often if she catches a glimpse of a child who resembles her own.

Judy is extraordinary. It would be extraordinary if she just got out of bed every morning. The death of her husband from hypothermia and delirium was so preventable, and so tragic because of shameful inaction. The slow motion of Annie's death was more horrifying and gut-wrenching than we can ever envision, too horrifying for Judy to fully describe aloud, even to me. On the worst of nights, she imagines that Ben did not die immediately. It is something Judy will grapple with for the rest of her life. Yet she does get up each morning, and she makes her lists, and she plans her day.

Judy has always considered her sense of humor and her sense of hopefulness her best allies in times of darkness. "I was always hopeful," she told me, "but even now I'm not sure what I was hoping for."

Initially Judy used her quilts to express her emotions, but her interests and activities have evolved as she develops a sense of well-being. She designed her own home, and for a period of time, using her engineering and design skills, she had a small development company, Benjamin Timon Ltd.

Her main involvement now is a business that revolves around flameworked glass beads, Annie Rose Ltd. (www.annierose.com). She sells Venetian glass rods, kilns, and supplies and tools for glass artists in New Zealand and Australia. She has designed a line of glass-beaded jewelry that is currently in several galleries in New Zealand, and she hopes her jewelry will show up in California in the next year.

The Wild Girls are ever present and still planning trips and activities, but they have given the final Outrageous Award to Isabelle.

Judy spends some of her evenings tutoring children in mathematics. She has also become a mentor in the New Zealand YWCA Future Leaders Programme for teenage girls. She has two little dogs, Sparkie and Elvis.

And me? I never planned on writing a book. There was always intense interest in Judy's story, and through the Sleavin Family Foundation we constantly received requests from authors, including some notable ones. Judy turned everyone down. Initially it was agonizing to even speak of the tragedy and the injustice. Recently she decided the time for a book had come, but she insisted that I be the person to write it. I was already aware of so much background information, she said, and because of the foundation, I had access to all the legal and investigative documents. I wasn't convinced until Judy told me she felt that she could tell me particular details she would not feel comfortable sharing with anyone else.

Still, it was a difficult process. Once, to break up the routine, we got in the car and just drove for three days. Some of the time we talked into a tape recorder, and some of the time we just whispered into the darkness. One evening, exhausted from crying, we stopped in a town with one restaurant and motel. We checked in, ate grilled cheese sandwiches, put each other's hair into pigtails, and entertained ourselves by singing Broadway songs and tap dancing. Our tears turned into hysterical laughter, and we finally slept for several hours. Then, considerably restored, we dragged ourselves back into the facts of those harrowing events.

Writing the book has been both a remarkable journey and an emotional minefield, causing me many sleepless nights. How could I not go through with this? Judy and Mike had always been so gracious to us. Over the years they shared meals, gifts, their home, their boat, and truly made me a member of the family when Annie Rose was born, honoring me as her godmother. Now perhaps I could do something in return. I am an avid reader, and books are precious to me. But books are bound pages, objects placed on a shelf. My goal, my most fervent desire, is that someday Judy will be able to point to this book and say that most of her grief and sorrows are now tangible, contained within the pages rather than within her soul, and that while her life is inseparable from the truth within these pages, it has diverged into her own personal, promising narrative.

I still love to travel, but I am no longer a blue-water cruiser.

In fact, I am no longer married, an unexpected 10-degree alteration of another sort. On the day I was banished by John, I went directly from the boat to Judy. This may seem an unlikely thing to do, since any despair on my part would be so minimal compared with the inhumanity and anguish she has had to endure. But no one avoids her. She continues to create a community of people who want to embrace life. People in her sphere make every effort to be kinder, wiser, funnier, more adventurous, and more compassionate because of the tone she has set. She has warped our perceptions in the most positive way. Through Judy's example, we want to take chances, to eliminate complacency and injustice, to be more courageous about the choices we make. We may need a grieving period or a time-out, but we know to take on life. And all Judy asks of anyone reading this book is to do the same, in memory of Michael Patrick, Benjamin Timon, and Anna Rose Sleavin.

## Four Distinct Personalities, but One Heart

*My love for you will*
*Never die*
*No one can take our*
*Dreams away*
*The depth of love can*
*Never be equaled*

*You are the stars*
*You are the glistening waves*
*You are the essence of my life*

*I see you in the clouds, I feel you in my heart*
*I promise to continue having adventures*
*I promise to fill my life with love*
*I promise to never compromise what is dear to me*

*My dreams of you keep my life*
*Full of love and adventures*
*You look down on me and smile*
*You protect me and guide me*
*You know we'll all be together*
*One day*

*Your love comforts me*
*I love you from the depth of my soul*
*A love that there are no words we know*
*We are one and always will be*
*Your love smoothes the road ahead of me*

JUDITH ANN SLEAVIN

# Acknowledgments

To Judith Ann Sleavin. This work would have been impossible without you. Without your truthfulness. Without your formidable courage. Without your trust. Without your loyal friendship. I can only humbly return it, with love and gratitude.

I had an early sense of how this story should be told, but as I surrounded myself with more and more documentation, the task seemed impenetrable. Personally, then, I am indebted to my sister, Susan. It was she who propelled me by telephoning me every day to command, "Write!"

I am also deeply beholden to my brother-in-law, Alan Roadburg, for his patience, guidance, and hours of technical expertise, and without whom I would not have entered the publishing arena.

I benefited enormously from the wisdom, sensibility, and astute editorial advice from Waverly Fitzgerald. Our discussions, fueled by large lattes, helped me sort out my thoughts and words. In my earliest drafts, Kathy Bradley, a meticulous copy editor, went beyond her role to provide me with good judgment and relevant suggestions.

More gratitude than I can express goes to my literary agent, Marly Rusoff, for her rare blend of professional excellence and tenderheartedness, to Michael Radulescu at the agency for championing me with gusto, and to Amy Einhorn, for her exceptional passion in bringing Judith Sleavin's spirit and story to a wide readership.

I am extremely grateful to the artist Margaret Davidson for creating the superb maps, and for her unrestrained enthusiasm for the project.

It would have been impossible to write this book without the access I had to all the documents, but it would have been impossible to review those thousands of pages without a firm knowledge base. From the inception of the Sleavin Family Foundation, and long before I had any intention of writing this book, numerous people were willing to share their professional expertise, research materials, and considerable skills to make sure that I understood essential issues. Members of the United States Coast Guard, members of the Council of American Master Mariners, and the following individuals contributed greatly to my level of comprehension and deserve special mention:

Donald J. Sheetz; Dr. Chris Gobey; Tom Linskey; Brian V. Dorsch; Captain Kip Carlson; CWO4 Eric Matthews, United States Coast Guard (ret.); Eugene Brodsky; Kay Rudiger; Captain Stephen Nadeau; Captain David Leach; Captain Robert Brownell; Ron Handy; Maria Russell; Pam Wall; Captain Derek McCann; Thomas Bayer; Carol Hasse; QMC Tom Rau; Captain David Smith; Ron Friedmann; Rob Hoffman; and Ken James.

With so much information gathered from New Zealand, and from worldwide shipping sources, I will have made unintended errors. The errors are mine alone, and not the product of anyone who assisted me.

I traveled to New Zealand three times to gather information and to interview principal and supporting characters. I am deeply indebted to Val Boag, Jigs Bradley, Judy Dempster, Diana Moratti, and Judy White for their gracious assistance and hospitality, humor, and thorough attention to my endless questions. I owe Ian Moratti many thanks as well, for arranging meetings, providing helpful information, and taking pertinent videos. I know how many tears were shed with the Wild Girls, and I am so grateful for their love.

I had the advantage of seeing the search and rescue area through the knowledgeable eyes of my helicopter pilot, Mr. J. Prickles de Ridder, who had kept his log book from 1995, when he made an attempt to retrieve Judy's dinghy at Deep Water Cove. And I had the opportunity to relive the search and rescue itself through the intact and objective memories of Sergeant Dave Palmer and Steve Simpson.

Annique Goldenberg and Kerry Rauber each provided invaluable help that allowed me to reconstruct the investigation and timing of the search and rescue. I am thankful for permission to reproduce their logs and diaries, and most particularly, am deeply grateful for their honesty in sharing very personal memories.

My thanks go to Daniel Levesque, COSPAS-SARSAT secretariat, for providing documents of the satellite system in 1995, and especially to Ron Wallace for providing the clarity and guidance to understand them. Thanks to Chris Wahler of ACR Electronics, for helping sort out 1995 EPIRB models.

Many topics in the book would have been incomplete without the helpful conversations, one-on-one interviews, or correspondence with the following people. I am indebted to them for their kindness and for the crucial information they provided. To the family members, I hope that you can forgive any pain I must have caused:

Catherine Sleavin, John and Kathi Sleavin, Sharon MacDonald, Colleen and Shannon Polley, Risa Graves, Maureen Lull, Peter and

Glenda Couch, Sid Hepi, Richard Witehira, Darryl Davis, Johnny Hepi, Mita Tipene, Efi Mosley, Dr. Charles Marmar, Dr. Loek Henneveld, Stephen Jones, and Jon Guzzwell.

Thanks go to Trisha O'Hehir, Birgit Westergaard, Judith Kimmerer, and Suzanne Fenton for reading drafts and offering useful suggestions; to Zanna Satterwhite, Holly Allen, and Laurie Radin for providing indispensable technical and organizational support; to Lisa Preston for conducting several overseas interviews on my behalf; to Lynda Lou Bouch for putting forward a good word well before I was ready; and to Amy Rennert for offering a novice some attention and guidance.

To the family and friends who cheered me on and sustained me through this process, I am forever grateful for your unfailing patience and encouragement. My eternal appreciation goes to:

Arlene Gladstone, Hamish Cameron, Birgit Westergaard, Norman Gladstone, Judy Kimmerer, Rob Kimmerer, Marilla Satterwhite, Skip Satterwhite, Bettie Rumberg, Ross Rumberg, Trisha O'Hehir, Marisa Kahn, Joel Wardinger, Alison Roadburg, Sheila Lieberman, Ann Phillips, Dr. Robert E. Holmberg, Jennifer Albright, Maralyn Crosetto, Jacqui Metzger, Holly Allen, James Piercey, Patricia Walter, Bea Gandara, Susan Finn, Suzie Kassen, Barry Kassen, Zanna Satterwhite, Stu Taylor, Jaida Kimmerer, Honna Kimmerer, Hamish Cameron Jr., Sylvia Gill, Beverly Moreland, Tina Castaldi, Francisco Nunez, Benjamin Benschneider, Tuckerman Esty, John Fitzgerald, Richard Bricker, Beau Hudson, Annie Hudson, Terri Sharp, Jeanette Logan, Alain Foucard, and, of course, Bud and Petey.

There are many other people who have enriched my life in a multitude of ways. I want to express apologies, although woefully inadequate, for all the friendships that have suffered. A legacy of the Sleavins: how harmful regrets can be and how important human connections are.

# Postscript

## *March 13, 2009*

It was a cool day with intermittent rain, but Judy and I, along with a group of friends, huddled together on a grassy mound waiting for the Welcoming Ceremony to begin. *Ten Degrees of Reckoning* had just recently been published, and we were in New Zealand. Now, purposely, we had arrived in the village of Rawhiti, in the Bay of Islands up north. Both Judy and I had been sent formal invitations by the Maori elders of Te Rawhiti Marae to celebrate the launch of the book, to commemorate Judy's rescue on their tribal land, and to remember Michael, Ben, and Annie Sleavin.

Our group was standing at the edge of the Marae, a complex of buildings that included a meetinghouse, a separate dining hall, and public space with a large expanse of lawn. We heard singing, and a pair of women, respected elders in the community, emerged from the meetinghouse. I didn't understand the words, but the melodic harmony was so evocative of Polynesian island countries I had visited. Then, with palm fronds, the women beckoned us forward to join the *iwi* (tribe) inside for formal speeches and storytelling.

Judy Sleavin's story is exceptionally significant to the people of Te Rawhiti Marae. In my recounting of Judy's ordeal to reach land, they were stunned to read she had been encouraged by their ancestor Nikora. Through oral narratives passed down, and written historical accounts, they were well-acquainted with Nikora, who, about two hundred years earlier, had been the chief of the Marae at Deep Water Cove—precisely where Judy struggled to get ashore. In the book, I inaccurately shortened their ancestor's name to *Niko*. Moreover, the whole scene of Chief Nikora at the shoreline and Maori tribesmen mingling about, I had ascribed to Judy's dehydration and exhaustion, and called her images the "hallucinations of hope."

I was not even gently refuted by the elders of Te Rawhiti Marae. I was embraced. I watched with grateful approval as the love poured out for Judy when she told her story to the hushed crowd.

We left the Marae to travel by boat to Deep Water Cove. Earlier in the week, two men had made a challenging hike in the rugged terrain to find the perfect rock for a plaque to be engraved with the names of Michael, Ben, and Annie. Judy and I were placed on a rocky precipice next to the plaque, which would be unveiled following further speeches and shared prayers for her family. It was extraordinarily emotional, but not the least unwelcome. I hoped for any ritual that might bring Judy further healing.

Judy walked across the sand and pebbles to show us where she first saw Nikora and the others. I looked around at the spectacular cliff face behind us, the forested ridges, and the tiny sheltered spot where Judy had sat and waited to be rescued. With the implausibility of that successful sighting heightened by the actual surroundings, I retold the story aloud. Dave Palmer, the spotter from the Cessna, had joined us for this dedication ceremony, and wept throughout. Even Dave, a devout Christian, an experienced policeman and an expert in search-and-rescue missions, was certain he saw and was guided by people other than Judy to this very secluded area.

We had started that morning as outsiders. As we prepared to leave, the hosts pressed each of our noses against theirs. This is called the *hongi* (a traditional greeting), where the *ha* or breath of life is exchanged and intermingled. It seemed very fitting in this place of genuine survival.

When we arrived at the Marae on the second day, there was a large framed picture of Michael, Ben, and Annie on the wall that held photographs and depictions of Maori ancestors. All cultural, social, educational, and economic concerns in this tight-knit community are taken very seriously, and it was a momentous decision to include the Sleavins, the only *Pakeha* (non-Maori) among their ancestors. But remarkably, it was Judy, not of their fold, who had brought past and present together.

This postscript is not about otherworldly visions. It is about people opening their hearts to one another through appreciation and unqualified acceptance. It is about the resident tribes of Te Rawhiti Marae considering Judy as *whanau*, or extended family. It is about Judy's looking forward and contributing to relationships that nurture and support her sense of kin. Judy will continue to learn the ways of this culture distinctive from her own, and the people of the Marae will discover more about Michael, Ben, and Annie. The memories of them, along with stories of the ancestors whose pictures share the wall, will be passed down through the generations. Judy has brought her own family to her adopted community, and to a new home.

# ABOUT THE AUTHOR

Hester Rumberg is an experienced ocean sailor, with thousands of nautical miles under her belt. After the tragedy befell the crew of the *Melinda Lee*, together with Judith Sleavin, she established the Sleavin Family Foundation, a nonprofit organization dedicated to promoting maritime safety throughout the world.

In her other life, Dr. Rumberg is a board-certified oral and maxillofacial radiologist. Hester was, and will always be, the godmother of Annie Rose Sleavin.

To contact the author, and for photographs, please go to: www.tendegreesofreckoning.com.